LETTERS OF AN INDIAN JUDGE
TO AN ENGLISH GENTLEWOMAN

Letters of an Indian Judge to an English Gentlewoman

Mandarin

A Mandarin Paperback
LETTERS OF AN INDIAN JUDGE
TO AN ENGLISH GENTLEWOMAN

First published in Great Britain 1934
by Peter Davies Limited

This edition published 1992
by Mandarin Paperbacks
Michelin House, 81 Fulham Road, London SW3 6RB

Mandarin is an imprint of the Octopus Publishing Group,
a division of Reed International Books Limited

A CIP catalogue record for this title
is available from the British Library
ISBN 0 7493 1208 4

Printed and bound in Great Britain
by Cox & Wyman Ltd, Reading, Berks

PUBLISHER'S NOTE

These letters were first published anonymously nearly sixty years ago with a publisher's note vouching for their authenticity.

In recent years some critics have suggested that the letters must have been edited or partially re-written before publication. Others have claimed that the entire book is a work of fiction written by the 'English Gentlewoman', now known to be the late Dorothy Black, author of over eighty novels.

In view of the inconclusive nature of the evidence this edition is published as non-fiction, leaving it open to each reader to judge the book's authenticity.

I

You must excuse a letter from somebody you may this morning not even remember. It is the lonely young man with the black face—beside the door—to whom you were so kind last night. I have only just returned from Cambridge, to Calcutta, and know no one here. It was a real ordeal to find myself at Government House, at such a large party, all alone in the world. I was busy wishing the floor would swallow me, or that perhaps death could arrive swiftly and quietly, when you came over and took pity on me, and so turned an evening that began as a nightmare, into a very pleasant one for me.

I had intended to call on you this morning, to thank you in person, but I learn that you have left Calcutta for Bombay.

Believe me,

Yours most sincerely and gratefully,

ARVIND NEHRA

II

I HAD not dared to hope that you would think it worth while to answer my letter, and so you can imagine with what pleasure I saw your handwriting this morning. It was most sweet of you to write to me. If ever I am in the same station with you again, I shall certainly come and see you, as you so kindly suggest, and only hope that by then you will not quite have forgotten the young man beside the door.

I am to go to Burma, on probation there. To a small station, Myosein, and it will, I fear, be some years before I return to India. I am delighted to find that I am to work under a Cambridge man, and that there are in Burma, many St. John's men also, which will make it pleasant for me, who am, at the moment, a little homesick for the West. I could have wished to start work, also, amongst my own people in India, there is so much to-day to be done, so much they have to be taught. But the Burman is, if not my brother, at least my cousin, though I know nothing of him and his customs as yet.

It is wonderful to be starting out on the threshold of life, at a time when everything is developing so fast, and life holds so many possibilities for us.

Does it really interest you to know of my home? We have lived in a large house on the outskirts of Pandila, a hot and sandy place, but to me beautiful because it is home. There is a large house with a flat roof upon which we played as children. From the roof you look for many miles across the country. We have eaten many sweetmeats (there is little discipline in the life of an Indian child) and amused ourselves well. The women quarrel a great deal, but that means little, and I look back with much happiness on those days. My Mother was very stout, but very kind, and we said our prayers regularly, all together in a family, in her rooms. Though the sanitary arrangements were rough and ready, only one of us has died of any disease.

My Father sent me to England when I was fifteen, first to a Tutor, where I lived in an English family. Then on to St. John's, Cambridge, which was also his old College. I was very happy there, and made many friends. It is a peaceful and beautiful place, and a quiet and dignified life that one learns of there. I worked very hard, but my work was to me a pleasure, because I am very ambitious and have great schemes for my country later on. When at last I said good-bye to England I was very sad. No Englishman could have watched those white cliffs fade, with greater regret. It is, I fear, many years before I shall again see the face of my kind Foster Mother. Nearly seven years of my life I spent there, and when I returned to India I found myself out of touch with her and many of her ways. I have missed, also, very much, the general friendliness to which I grew accustomed at College. I have noticed the change already when I came on to the ship. Between me and the other passengers a great gulf was fixed, and there was no one to hold a friendly hand across it.

But I shall bore you with my long letter, and then you will not write to me again, and that is the last result I wish to achieve. I go by mail steamer to Burma to-morrow and my address will be c/o the Chief Courts, Myosein, Lower Burma. Please, if ever you have any time to spare, will you remember again the lonely young man beside the door, who will now be a lonely young man amongst the rice fields?

III

WITH a cargo of Buddhist Priests, goats, dorians and mangoes, we sailed away. In four days we came to Burma, a very flat country. So flat I cannot tell what there is to 'stop the sea walking right over it and wiping it out, but this it does not do. It is a pleasant country, light-hearted and green, there are large flowers upon the trees, and the very moon seems larger than usual, and of a festive appearance suggestive of gala. And always, from round the corner, there comes curious music, or the echoing note of a bell. You feel as if you were taking part in some Theatricals. That presently the curtain will fall and the actors go home.

But the curtain does not fall, and the play goes on and on. Life here proceeds as gaily by night as by day, indeed many people seem to have no fixed hours of repose. It was one o'clock in the morning when, proceeding down a by-street, I found all the houses lit with candles, and everybody working at making umbrellas. Here and there, in a corner grandpapa snatched forty

winks, but in no time he was up again, and work
ing with the others. The umbrellas they had
finished bordered the road outside, to dry, like
large mushrooms born of a nocturnal shower.

In Burma, they are always having great fun,
and in most cases they find some Religious excuse
for having it. Upon the Pagoda slopes I see
no end of a beano is prepared. Booths of
jugglers, and sweetmeat sellers, and side shows
of every sort, and in the centre of it all there is
an Elephant, many more times larger than life
size, made out of bamboo and coloured paper.
Presently I discover that all this is because of
the death of a famous Priest. That he dies only
six months ago, is nothing. They have him
there, pickled in Honey, and at the moment he
reclines on a small shelf inside the elephant.
To-morrow they will put a light to it, and the
whole show will go up in flames. What fun to
have such a jolly and splendid funeral. Only a
Burman could think of it.

I have spent a very amusing evening going over
the side shows, watched some curious dancing
and part of a play interminable as only plays of
the East can be. And all this, because a Priest
has died, six long months ago.

I have always been told the backbone of the

British Empire is the Middle Class. The back-bone of Burma, it is bamboo, and coloured paper. Not only was the elephant composed of it, but also the stalls at this Fair, and the lanterns that decorate the landscape like a smile everywhere. All bamboo and coloured paper. And sometime going through a village, I have come upon a very splendid castle, all towers and turrets and little windows and enchanting railings—and that is all bamboo and coloured paper, too. Behind it there is nothing but the small mat hut of the local weaver. But for a little while, until the winds blow, or the rains come, he can have all the illusions of living in a palace. And I said to myself, after all it is not more unlike than some of civilization's fantastic consolations.

Consider what fun. To make for yourself from bamboo and coloured paper a more than life-sized elephant or tiger, and to sit inside, entirely carefree and with nothing important to do, and play the drum, or the reed pipe, or some clappers. Is that not a pleasant life?

The only solid thing about this Fair was the Golden Pagoda. This rears itself up against a background of sky and stars. I would very much like to paint a picture of it for you.

They tell me many precious stones and much

gold was buried beneath the Pagoda at the time of its building, but the Burmese gentleman who told me this laughed happily, and said he doubted whether much of it was left there now, but they hoped for the best. On top of the Pagoda sits a small umbrella, also studded with precious stones. On the platform are many statues of Buddha seated in various positions. They are mostly a little tumble-down and troubled with the results of sparrows. There is a great bell close by, which you must strike after offering up your prayer, and your prayer is wafted away on the echo, until it arrives at the throne of the Great Ones.

Standing up there in the sunshine and the stillness, I think again of Westminster Abbey, which I love very dearly. For there one finds the same stillness, the same stone statues, only they are of gentlemen with beards and swords. All manner of men surround their Gods with mystery and with stone figures, each to their different taste. Somewhere, I suppose, there is one God. We all approach him in our several ways, and fashion Him in our likeness. We build Him temples of our fond imaginings. Whilst all the time no doubt He remains somewhere without, and laughs kindly at our toys.

I visit there also the Gymkhana Club, where many people were seated round small tables, and a band was played by soldiers in uniform that must indeed have been hot. But here I remained the lonely young man apart, and no one came to my rescue.

Life, I perceive, is not for me to be as easy and as pleasant as it was in Cambridge. I had under-rated the importance and the magnitude of the colour question, which strangely enough, England almost allows one to forget. I have received over there so much hospitality and kindness, but now I begin to understand that it was because I was a guest. That here, it will not be quite the same. That there are adjustments to make, before one finds one's feet again.

If you can guess out of your kindness, a little of my loneliness, you will also imagine some of the pleasure it gives me to find that after all I am not entirely cut off from England and the pleasant days I have known, as long as you will, from time to time write to me.

IV

HERE I am, after four days upon a riverine steamer on which there were also many goats, Chinamen, and dorians. Also a Scotch Captain and Chief Officer, who indeed spend a queer life, isolated as they are in these backwaters, apart from all their own kind. We have our meals together, and then I notice a curious thing. Although these two white men are the only two white men, they do not speak. They refrain entirely from addressing one another, and later I learn that they hate one another very much, and have not spoken save where it was necessary for their work, for years.

Myosein is a small huddle of houses upon the river bank, with the inevitable Pagoda reached by the usual steps beneath a corrugated iron roof, painted vermilion. If the Indian builds with corrugated iron, it looks messy. But the Burman paints it crimson in a dull shade, and arranges it so cunningly that it is beautiful and for this I must take off my hat to him.

Beside the Pagoda there is the Hpoongyi

chaung or school kept by the Priests. It is falling to pieces but a stout creeper lashes together much of it that must otherwise go. It is raised on sticks because at high tide the river rises under it, which on the whole is a good thing. There are many dogs, goats, cows, cats and hens living all about the place, and the effect is picturesque if smelly. Very different to those peaceful villages I have grown accustomed to, in the West, with their Sabbath quiet and tended gardens. Here it is like a print by Hogarth, with lots of amusing detail, a hint of squalor, the whole macabre.

Life here is nothing, and death, it is nothing also. To-day I meet it behind the door. I have been inspecting some traps to drive myself about in, and yesterday visit a Chinaman who has some for sale. Protruding from behind the door, I see a foot. At the time, I think nothing of it. It is someone who, turning day into night as is the fashion of these people, snatches forty winks. But this morning, when I go back to clinch my bargain, there is still the foot, in the same position, so I asked the Chinaman regarding it a little uneasily, and he laughed a whole lot and said, "Oh, yes, that was quite all right." It was only his Father who had died of the plague, and they awaited even then the arrival of the coffin.

[17]

I asked the Chinaman if he himself was not afraid of catching the complaint. He replied that he had had no time to think about things like that, as trade at the moment was very brisk.

There are many diseases in the town and the neighbourhood is not too wholesome. In the matter of houses also, I have not been fortunate. There is a house that goes with my job, but it is inhabited by an Englishman, and his wife, and a small child. Indeed I have not the heart to insist on his giving it back to me, also I am not convinced that my insistence would do much good. I begin, you see, to know my place.

This house that should be mine is in a good place, standing on high ground, beside the golf course. There is the open jungle around, so that some of the fresher of the breezes can be got in the evening.

As for me I have a small house in the Bazaar. One can picture that they have said to themselves, "He is an Indian and will not care where he lives." And so upon this matter of the exchange I have not been consulted. It seems to me a little odd that it does not strike people, we learn in England many things as well as those from our lesson books, and take on also some liking for the sanitary ways of the West. But I

see it always in the eye of such Hostesses as are
bound to entertain me from time to time, and
who ask me to dine, and then grow weak with a
terror lest I shall not know how to behave at the
table. Shall I, perhaps, add to my visiting card
in small letters these words, "Warranted Trained
to the House."

Well, I must tell you of my new abode. It is on
the banks of one of those small streams that is
little but an open drain, carrying as it does most
of the refuse from most of the town, down into
the river. After my rooms looking down on to the
pleasant waters of the river Cam, I found it a
little depressing. Along come the bodies of dogs
and of cats, and the scourings of the local
abattoirs and much garbage. I have done what
I can to this side of the house, by completely
blocking up this side of the house, leaving open
for air and for view, only that one which looks
on to the Bazaar.

The Bazaar is built mostly of corrugated iron
with small wooden tumble-down buildings here
and there amongst it. All very low they are, and
have the air of squatting in the dust. Within it is
also very colourful and smelly. There are goats
and lepers and passers-by in creaking bullock
carts all day long, and Burmese boys playing

upon reed pipes, so that I need never have a dull moment. Opposite to my house there is a large store bearing these words, "Very Good Chinese Selly Shop Photographer and Dentist".

The Courts where I go daily are buildings of yellowish brick, painted inside a pale green, so that on arriving there one has the sensation of inserting oneself into a melon that is no longer as fresh as it one day was. I have often wondered why they are so fond, the Government, of buildings of brick. It is not a medium very suited for this climate, being slow to cool down, also very heavy to fall upon one, in an earthquake.

In the Compound of the Courts there is a Lock Up which has shocked me very much. Small it is, with bars in the front, like a dog's kennel, and inside it are packed more men than there is room for. When I pass they are holding on to the bars, looking through like animals. Such a thing would not be tolerated these several hundred years, in England. It is a disgusting sight. I only hope it acts as a deterrent. It would certainly deter me.

V

THANK you for a very kind letter, which has cheered me up a whole lot. You wish to know something of the people with whom I work, and so I shall tell you. My Chief is the Commissioner, Mr. Cambourne. He is a Cambridge man, but he is not inclined to be very friendly with me and I fancy he has been more than a little annoyed that it is an Indian who is sent down to him and not a young Englishman. So I do what I can to live down my dark face, and trust in time to succeed.

Mr. Cambourne is married to a Burmese lady, which also makes his position a little difficult, for many of the people in the station like this as little as he likes me, and so there is some tension. She is a charming person, very small and dainty, and they have so many children that although they keep two gharries, some have to walk.

For D.C. there is a young man whose name is Mr. Nigel Hill. He was at Oxford, and he is brilliantly clever, and he treats me as if I was a dog. A nice dog, quite well behaved. I can be certain of punctual bones from him, I feel, but between us there is no point of contact that I can discover as yet. I continue looking, however, with hopefulness.

There is also a policeman, of whom one sees little, a Doctor, who is a Eurasian but pretends he is Irish. That finishes meantime the Government community. Some way out of the station there are many Rice Mills, with bungalows and gardens, and wives and children there, a large community of their own, with many dinner parties, tennis, and dancing. Besides them, yet another community arises. They have Engineers, subordinates, and assistants.

Each one of these communities has their Club. Each Club is armed and fortified against the other Clubs. For a stranger it is a little hard to understand. By the recent amendment of a bye-law I am now admitted to the Government Club, but I have only been there once. In the Scotch Club, which is for Engineers and so on, only Scotch is spoken, and the Club, I gather has to be rebuilt each day following St. Andrew's night, for the Scotsman is very warlike in joy. Then there is the Town Club, to which the Eurasians belong if they cannot pretend not to be Eurasian successfully enough to get into any other Club. For it seems to me to be the desire of everybody to get into another Club from the one to which their state of life has called them; the aim of the other Club to keep them out. England it seems, also has her caste system, as difficult, as unovercomeable, as any of ours.

The dark daughter of Mr. Palmerston, a contractor, is shortly to marry Mr. Malkin, who is an assistant in a Rice Firm. Then she, automatically, will become a member of that Club to which her Father, Mother, and Sisters· cannot belong. That is to say, unless Mr. Malkin gets the sack because he is marrying her, as some think more than likely. Indeed, Mr. Malkin is in a clove hitch with his dark Guinevera! For if he does not marry her, then all decent men must say he is a cad, and if he does marry her, half his community will certainly cut him, and he may even get the sack.

Wherever men go, they take their complications with them. Here upon the desolate banks of the river so far from any civilization, surely one might have looked for peace.

Once I had the temerity to look into the windows of the Ladies Room at the Government or most exclusive Club. What did I see there? Seated alone at a table beneath an oil lamp that guttered, one very old lady. She keeps the Home for Sailors, though not many sailors go there. (It is from a less desirable quarter of the Bazaar they have for ever to be sought for and dug out.) A little acid, she looked, and there was some jet in her bonnet, as if recently she had enjoyed a funeral. Only once have I spoken to this lady, and then she has regaled me with accounts of all the interments that have taken place during the year, and told me who made a lovely corpse, and whom the reverse. Beneath the guttering lamp she read an illustrated paper three weeks old.

Will no one inform the Mothers and Sisters and other relations of Guinevera Palmerston that they are not missing much?

A parcel has just come for me. I opened it and found your books. I do not know how I am going to thank you for your goodness and kindness to me. It is a day's march to get books here, and these come as a perfect godsend. I shall enjoy reading them so much and they will take me back to England, her quiet villages and sweet scented fields, and help me to forget for a while the Bazaar and the passing bullock carts and the festive sounds for ever emerging from the Chinese Selly Shop.

Yes, we have a Library here, attached to the

Government Club. I have looked into it once or twice, but find only ancient novels and many detective stories dealing with many crimes. In one book also I find half a poached egg and some ants.

Please accept again my very grateful thanks, and appreciation of your thoughtfulness for me.

VI

YOUR charming letter duly reached me and I enjoyed so much getting news of you and I hope that the Colonel Sahib likes his new post, and you your new house and surroundings. I, too, wish that I could get some riding here, but there is not much chance of it. There are only rice fields and jungle too thick to be of much use to anyone.

You will be interested to hear of a change that has brought me a good friend. The Commissioner Mr. Cambourne was transferred some months ago, and in his place has come Mr. Chelston. Mr. Chelston is six foot four in height, and a very charming person. I feel the need of stilts to raise myself to his level, and not only physical stilts also mental ones. From the beginning he has been friendly towards me, and seems unconscious of that difference between us as men, of which I have lately been made so painfully aware. His coming will make a great difference to my stay here, and also I feel that I shall get on much better with my work, under him.

I wish that I could draw you a picture of Mr.

Chelston to give you some idea of him. He is extremely thin, with shoulders almost as wide as the top of a Government House dining table. But in face he has something of that sweetness and quietness I have always found in the faces of men who are true scholars, and sometimes, only more rarely, in Bishops. He has fair hair that curls, and is almost exactly the shade of the tussore silk suits which he always wears, and which always appear to remain immaculately clean even in this unsalubrious climate.

With Mr. Cambourne there was a something that prevented his impressing others very favourably, and also he had much difficulty in restoring order. I have thought it might be because he had lost respect in marrying a Burmese wife. When he wished for silence, there was often much shouting and rapping on desks, and often I have seen him beat and kick people.

When Mr. Chelston arrives, he brings his silence with him. I have not yet heard him raise his voice, but with one long look he can strike terror into the malefactor's heart that is more pungent than any kick. They fear him very much, but also they love him. They call him the Bo Gyi, which means the Very Large European. I also love him and admire him very much.

[27]

When he saw what manner of young man it was he had on probation under him, his face did not fall. On the contrary he appeared to be pleased to hear I had been to Cambridge and of my time there, and he knew some of the Tutors at my College.

When he saw the house I lived in, he was very angry, and when Mr. Chelston is angry things happen with great swiftness, although he does not say much. It appears that this English family who have had my house have no right whatever to it, being no longer in the Service at all, but retired.

I implored Mr. Chelston not to make any unpleasantness about it, as it would increase my unpopularity, to which he replied: "Do not fall into the error of believing that patience is a virtue."

"The whole duty of man, Nehra, is not to shirk unpleasantness. The path of least resistance leads to the garbage heap of despair."

So now I have my own house, and look out into the Jungle and get clean breezes in the evening, nor am I forced any longer to listen to the festive sounds emerging from the Selly Shop, or the low fights of many dogs after sundown.

Mr. Chelston was sent here especially to make

a drive to clear up the rice thieving that has been going on in this district for many years. Mr. Chelston, it seems, is very good at clearings up, and that I can well imagine. He is to take firm steps to put it down, but when I ask him what steps, he rubs his hands, and looks at me and laughs, and tells me that sufficient unto the day is the evil thereof. It is in January and February that these matters are at their worst, and so no doubt Mr. Chelston will take his steps, whatever they are to be, then. At that time of year, the Rice Firms give out large money advances to their Brokers, who go to the Jungle, taking with them gigs in which to bring back the rice. The procedure of the thieves is to hold up these gigs and rob them, either of the money or the rice. It has become quite a flourishing industry, and has to be stopped. There is a whole colony of thieves some twenty miles down the river but the difficulties of running them to earth are great. Firstly because they operate in boats, and have all the Jungle to hide in, and the jungle, like the law, is on the side of the malefactor in most cases. Although it is now known quite well who is at the head of this gang responsible for many dozens of murders, nothing can be done about it, and no evidence comes; for if anyone opposes them,

he is knifed and his body washed down to Myosein later, upon the flood tide. Unless definite
evidence can be got, and the men caught red-
handed, nothing can be done. And how can they
be caught red-handed? They are much too clever
for it.

This is a great difficulty. We know at the
present time of two men who have committed
certain crimes. There is no shadow of doubt about
it. But because we did not see them doing it,
we cannot touch them. This may be an excellent
law in a civilised country. In the Jungle, I find
it a farce.

Mr. Chelston owns that he also finds it a farce,
but he added that he himself always tempered
Justice with discretion, so I asked him how, and
he replied:

"Never mind, have a cigarette."

Life for me is much pleasanter now, for I get
some golf and many interesting talks, and we go
for walks together. Also Mr. Chelston takes me
on tour with him where I learn a great deal of
the workings of this complicated machinery of
Government. I often dine with him, and he with
me, and with him, I sometimes go into the Club.

Such is the force of personality that when I go
to the Club with Mr. Chelston, everyone is very

nice to me, and I do not stand alone beside the door. I sometimes make up a Bridge four, a thing I have not had a chance of doing since I left Cambridge. Mr. Chelston appears to possess that curious faculty of making other people sink their own differences meantime, and let down their fortifications against each other. Even in the matter of Clubs it is the same. He will go in one evening from one Club to the other, and always they are pleased to see him, and me because I am with him, and so we spend a pleasant evening.

If there were more people like him out here, how much easier life would be, how few of those problems would arise that loom so largely upon the horizon out here just now, that I am always hearing of with such misgivings. To be feared and respected alone, it is not enough when the final test comes. It is only the hand that holds in friendship, which in time one does not desire to shake away.

VII

How strange that you should know Mr. Chelston. I gave him your message, and when I told him that I also knew you, he said that I was fortunate in my friends.

That is a thing I also have been feeling of late very keenly. Life has settled down so pleasantly for me here now, and I am so keen on my work and see so much that can be done with determination and perseverance, although I now begin to see that the new heaven and the new earth that I had an idea of making out here when I left Cambridge was, perhaps, too ambitious an undertaking altogether.

It is so kind of you to take an interest in this place and our doings, and I was so pleased when you told me you thought I wrote a good letter and had taken you to Myosein so that you felt you could know your way about if ever you came here. It gives me some of the greatest pleasure that I have to-day, to write to you, and to feel that you are a friend of mine. Living in England gives us a taste for the friends, the conversations, the sort of life that once we leave her, we can only in very rare cases ever hope to have again. It makes us wish to meet, as equals, people who from the beginning make it plain they cannot regard us as such. It is all a matter of adjustments, but adjustments often pinch. I do not feel any bitterness about it, for I see that these things must be. Like all young people, I hoped for too much.

Last night again the Langholm Rice Company sent words that their gigs had been interfered with, and another of their men killed. To-morrow his body will come down on the flood tide. Two of the crew escaped with their lives, and Mr. Chelston has just seen them. They have told him again the name of the man who did the killing and again it is the same man we have heard of so often before, but can get no more direct evidence about.

After they had gone I found Mr. Chelston very pleased rubbing his hands.

"Nehra," he said to me, "the time has come to act."

But when I said, "Act how?" he replied, "Never mind," and looked pleased as a Bishop giving a Benediction. He then proceeded to give me some strange orders, which I have to carry out without questions. I learnt then that he himself would be away for one or two days and I am not to tell anyone that he is away but to say he is indisposed meantime, and deal with all eventualities myself, pretending I have instructions from him, upstairs.

All this I find very mystifying, and also I am a little afraid. It is with much uneasiness that I learn he is going all alone, and I entreated him to allow me to accompany him, because I feared his errand would be dangerous.

He laughed at that, and said it would be dangerous for me, but not for him and would not discuss it with me any more.

The Langholm gigs went out to-night with more money, with other gigs in tow to bring back the rice in, and with them went Mr. Chelston. Only one thing he tells me, and that is that he intends to anchor for the night, off the village where it is well known to us these thieves are in hiding. After my dear friend has departed, I search anxiously in the safe, and find to my horror that his revolver is still there, and that he has gone on this errand taking only his walking stick, which seems to me madness. For a while I meditated following him in the motor boat to take him his revolver, but feared this would disclose that which he wished to remain secret, and so I refrained and spent a wretched day of anxiety. In the evening I went to the Club to pass away the time, but Mr. Chelston not being with me, I remained unhailed, beside the door. Then I tried the Engineers' Club and saw only a young man with reddish hair who called to me:

"What do you want here, Black Face?" And is it not sad, no bears came out to eat him up, as they did for Elijah.

So then I came home, and here I am, reading over your last kind letter, and trying to forget my anxiety by writing to you.

VIII

I BREATHE once more. My kind friend, Mr. Chelston, returned from his strange and secret trip in good spirits, looking sunburnt and well after three days' rest from his files, and the melon-like interior of the Court House.

"How now?" I asked him all in a hurry, "did you see the Budmarsh?"

Mr. Chelston nodded his head. He said "Yes."

"And what did you do?"

Mr. Chelston replied: "He has been disposed of."

"How? Disposed of? Have you, then, brought him back to be tried?"

Mr. Chelston regarded me very wisely and very kindly, just as many years ago my own Father regarded me when I peppered him with foolish questions.

"All I can tell you is just that, Nehra. He has been successfully disposed of. We shall be troubled by him no more."

Then he laid a hand on my shoulder, and said:

"The successful master of a machine knows at

once when that machine has temporarily broken down, Arvind, and he Takes Steps. I have just taken steps, in the Jungle. That is all. Have a cigarette?"

So I had a cigarette, and wondered greatly. And I find it is true, the gang is now broken up. Since that time, two months ago, we have no more reports from any of the mills. Sometimes I am eaten up with curiosity and beg my good friend to let me into this secret of his efficacy with thieves. All Mr. Chelston will say on such occasions is:

"I never chips nor cracks. When I breaks I smashes utterly."

Already it becomes very hot here. In the trees the Hot Weather Bird calls and calls, like one heralding a disaster. Flying foxes hang head downwards in bunches in the trees around the Courts, and the smell of them reaches into our office, so rank it is. All the world is now eating mangoes and throwing away the stones so that the ground is littered with them, and after the mangoes come many flies, and after the flies, the cholera which rages here every season without any failing.

Very sordid, very dirty a place is Myosein, and yet along the river banks it is beautiful. Down on the tide come water hyacinths in purple and green masses, like pretty eiderdowns of flowers floating over the water. The sunset paints the river the colour of opals and in it the golden pagoda mirrors itself, a smaller replica of the golden pagoda in Rangoon. White paddy birds come winging along over the river, and for a little while the dirt and squalor of the bazaar fades from the mind.

To-day I went to a hanging.

It was Mr. Chelston who took me.

"One of these days you will have to attend these things on your own. Better learn the ropes now," he said to me. So we repaired to the jail. It is a sad place of brick, clean inside and standing amongst many acres of vegetables, which the convicts themselves bring up by hand. I do not think that prison is much deterrent to the Burman, nor as far as that goes, to the less educated Indian. There is no shame attached to a sojourn there, and you get free and good food at regular intervals. Only the lack of women and of tobacco are regarded as privations. Many of the older Burmans, I learn, hastily commit some offence when they are liberated, so that they may return there again.

I was taken to inspect the kitchen and see and

taste some of their food. It was very good. It is one of the tasks of a Government official, to go and inspect the jail regularly and to make himself familiar with their food.

I spoke to several Indians there. They seemed very contented, save for this one complaint, that tobacco and women were much missed. In the jail I noticed there were no Chinamen, but this, Mr. Chelston assured me, was not due to virtue, but cunning, as no Chinaman ever got caught, being much too clever. They continue to flourish and prosper until in due course they are rich enough to retire from business and become Members of the Legislative Council, and more often than not, are Knighted in a very short time.

For myself I had no wish to participate at a hanging and asked Mr. Chelston why this was necessary. He then informed me of a strange custom amongst these people. They do not greatly object to being hanged so long as there is a Government official present at the hanging. If no official is present, there may be a great deal of fuss. And the reason for this is a simple one. You can hang a man's body and so be rid of it. But you cannot hang his soul. There his soul is, and must remain always in the jail, unless given special permission to depart by a Government Official or other Authority.

The Burmese people are very particular about this, and Mr. Chelston told me how only the previous week the wife of Ba Hla, our clerk, deceased of cholera, had arrived in the office to ask him to dismiss her husband officially, as although his body was indeed dead, his soul still remained over the Petty Cash book because as yet he had not had the official sack.

Whereupon Mr. Chelston gave her a paper which said that Maung Ba Hla had been a good and faithful servant and left the situation through no fault, but with the Commissioner's full permission and consent, and so the lady departed very happy taking away the soul of her husband with her.

All this Mr. Chelston told me while we waited for our hanging. The prisoner had done many cruel actions and looked at the last a trifle ashamed of himself. As he stood upon the gallows, Mr. Chelston raised his topee in his polite manner and said in his quiet voice:

"Maung Lu Gale, committed to Death for murder, you may leave this jail with my full permission and consent." After which Maung Lu Gale did so.

IX

I WAS so much interested to hear of the birth of your small son, and so much touched that you should find time to write and tell me about it. To be the mother of a son, that is a wonderful thing. To Indian women there are no words so beautiful as those which tell them they have brought a man child into the world. Since in their inmost hearts, all women have so much in common, you also will know something now of what this means. Though, of course, I know you must never say so. In England I have noticed that one must love all one's children the same. Also I have noticed, one never does.

May I, perhaps, one day have a snap-shot? I would like so much to make his, and renew my, acquaintance with you.

The Rains are upon us. Cholera has been very bad this season and rages in the Bazaar and we take many measures against it. To-morrow Mr. Chelston takes me with him by launch some way into the Jungle, where there is lately trouble about the collection of taxes. I have spent pleasant months since last writing you, in going about with him, and have made much progress in my understanding of the work.

This launch trip will be our last of the season, for in the Rains we do not as a rule tour. We remain at home, and struggle with our files. I cannot ever explain to you, in all its pathos, this business of files. About everything there is a written report and a docket, and now the mass is already so large that no human eye could possibly peruse it all, and still it grows. In many offices I have seen files almost to the ceiling. I have often thought it, but did not very much like to put it into words for myself. Lately Mr. Chelston has done so for me.

"What we want, Arvind," he said, "is a good fire to do away with all files and precedents. Then we could begin all over again, profiting by our later experience, and we should do much better."

Indeed there is altogether too much initialling and writing, and looking up the decision someone else made in 1892. For after all, might that decision not have been a wrong one? Indeed it seems to me that the machine is becoming too complicated and the out-turns smaller and smaller, because all the energy we have is taken up seeing to the works of the machine instead of the results.

Here I am disturbed because there is a hubbub in my garden. It is a snake. With many loud cries and with ten-foot bamboos, my servants, fourteen in number, flung themselves into him, and belaboured him. When I hasten to see, Lo! it was such a small snake, and after all, not poisonous. The snake that would have eaten rats.

May I wish your small son much happiness and prosperity, and yourself a quick return to good health and much pleasure in your Motherhood. If I could have come to his christening, as the God Parents came to the christening of Snow White, only one thing would I wish for him. That would be that he might inherit his Mother's kindly heart, and then I think most other things he wishes will come to him.

x

IT is some time since I wrote, and I apologise for being so long in answering your last letter, but you will understand what it has been to me. I think my last letter was when we were just starting for our trip to the Jungle. When I went to see Mr. Chelston the evening before, it was easy to realize he was not well, and I begged him then to postpone this journey, but Mr. Chelston only laughed at me and said one must never let pleasure interfere with business. In vain I pointed out that to take care of the health was not pleasure, he replied only no, that it was boredom, and so we started just the same.

In the pouring rain we started, and were carried down stream at a great rate upon the flood of the river which ran with us. Although he has said nothing to me, I am aware that Mr. Chelston is not at all well, and again I besought him to return to where we could get the Doctor. He replied that if there was one thing that would make him feel really worse, it would be the sight of the Myosein Doctor, who is of dark colour, but calls himself an Irishman. And he laughed at me and said, "Arvind, I have never before suspected you of being a bit of an old woman." And so my dear friend would not listen to anything I said, and we continued to forge on through much rain and bad weather. In the evening, Mr. Chelston took some medicine and seemed a little better. Also I made him drink some brandy, for in this climate it is very good for the inside, and I did not like the look of my dear friend even at that time, being frightened in my heart as to what it might be.

In the night I hear noises from his cabin, and going there in haste, find him very ill indeed. Even then he would not let me give orders to turn the launch. "I shall be all right in the morning," he said. But before long I have to give him more brandy, and then I took matters into my own hands, and gave orders that the launch should make all speed for Myosein again, for at Myosein there is the Hospital and proper drugs and we had nothing. I sat with him all the rest of the night. Towards morning, Mr. Chelston became so ill that he said to me:

"I fear you are right and that we must go back." Then I told him for many hours already we have been going back full steam ahead. By the look in his eyes I know that he is now glad that I have done this. I gave him much brandy and got hot-water bottles to warm him, for about this time he grew very cold, and so I became certain that it was the cholera, but still comforted myself, because with proper care and nursing a man need not die and I had calculated we should be in Myosein by noon, for the tide had turned and was carrying us along fast.

We might have made it as I thought, but towards eleven o'clock ran on to a sand bank, carried there by the floods. We remained stuck there meantime, and Mr. Chelston, when he heard that, laughed.

"You see," he said, "I am to be spared that tiresome Doctor after all, Nehra." And then, because he saw I could not keep back my tears, he said, "Silly boy. No man can live for ever. I have had my pickle of fun, and of hard work, and have no complaints, though I own I would have liked to finish my course . . ."

"You will be all right. Soon we shall get free and arrive in Myosein," I told him, but by the way he smiled at me then, I knew he knew that I lied. So he kept his hand on my knee and said many things to me which I shall never forget.

"Given a fair chance, you should go a long

way," he said to me. "You will see much that will shock you and much that will disappoint you, and many hard things. You will hear renegade conversation in high places, but the right is there, if you can find it and follow it. An honest man has no superiors," he said, also. And "the English caste system is much more complicated and difficult to follow than yours. Once a Sweeper always a Sweeper. But with us—tomorrow the Sweeper may be walking upon the face of his master. This we call progress. You must have patience with these things. I like your country," he said. "I think she is in for the devil of a lot of trouble, and those who sponsor her cause most warmly will do her the greatest harm. People like yourself who have tolerance and understanding of the problems of other peoples, and the customs of other parts of the world, can be of much use to her."

Then, perhaps because I cannot restrain my sorrow, Mr. Chelston changed his subject and said:

"Shall I tell you something, Nehra? Would you like to know what happened to those rice thieves that were disposed of? It will not matter if I tell you, now."

He told me how he had remained himself on

board after they anchored for the night, enclosing the crew below. How he seated himself with his back to the mast so that the gig had the appearance of being in the usual emptiness that reigns when the crew go to sleep, and so he waited.

In due course a long boat put out from the bank in the usual fashion, and they were boarded, and the first man who climbed on board is this man we have for months been trying to get hold of, and following him is his well known lieutenant. Mr. Chelston waited until they were on board. Then he stood up to his full height, and I can well imagine that scene on the river. By moonlight when not expected, Mr. Chelston's full height would certainly be a little alarming. He took one after the other by the scruff of the neck, and knocked their heads together. Then swinging them round he let them go, and with a splash they disappeared. The remainder of the thieves, screaming that the devil was upon the gig, made off as fast as they could, in such haste that they too capsized and were last seen struggling in the water and what became of them Mr. Chelston said he did not know nor care.

"You will find in the life of every community

there are times when swift action is better than conferences. The world is running too much to talk," said Mr. Chelston. "A sock on the jaw is often worth five files in the office."

Then he smiled at me again, and quoted his favourite saying:

"I never chips, nor cracks. What I breaks I smashes utterly."

Shortly after that he died, and I could do nothing. Oh, my good friend, I cannot tell you what that meant to me. Indeed he spoke the truth, for himself also, with his incessant work, his never taking any care of himself, he smashed utterly. So has the country lost a valuable Servant, and I, my best friend. I shall never forgive myself that I did not turn the launch without consulting him, and make for Myosein the previous evening. This was indeed an occasion when swift action would have been better than endless talk, and lamentably I failed.

We arrived back at six in the evening. At daybreak the next morning, Mr. Chelston was buried in the small English churchyard here, where there are so many graves that have neither name nor stone. I went early to see all was in readiness, and there I found the elderly lady who keeps the Sailors' Home, waiting at the grave-side, with some jet in her bonnet. Always I suspected that she loved above all things an interment, and I am proved right.

They gave Mr. Chelston a military funeral, the Railway Volunteers, which are all the soldiers we have, turning out as best they could, for many of them have not drilled for long. So we marched from the Hospital to the Cemetery. I wished I might have helped to carry my friend, but feared to suggest this, as I was not asked. The Railway Volunteers blew the Last Post and fired a volley across the grave, and one of the Volunteers, not being sure of his rifle, fired too soon and nearly blew some of the jet off the bonnet of the old lady who is so fond of funerals. The Military part of the funeral was not successful, but they have all done their best. After that, they marched back with their band playing, Hold Your Hand Out Naughty Boy, whilst I remained alone behind.

There was only one consolation about the morning. That was for me the thought of how amused Mr. Chelston would have been if he could have seen his own funeral and seen the Doctor wearing, for the occasion, his famous top hat of a shape now no longer known.

Life has seemed very empty since. I am always

coming in my walks to places we visited together, and in my work to files that are annotated in his hand, and being made to realize, at every turn, how much poorer the world now is.

XI

Do you subscribe largely to Foreign Missions? Perhaps if you do I shall hurt your feelings a little. Of all the bells that call to prayer in this place, the only one unanswered is the English Church bell. The Roman Catholic Church is well filled, its Good Sisters minister to the poor and to the children. The Baptist Mission flourishes a little way down the river, for it employs many, has rice mills and saw mills, and in short goes in for Salvation, and ten per cent. All along the river bank at sunrise and at sunset the prayer mats are spread and worshippers prostrate themselves to the rising or the setting sun. On the steamers that ply along the river, the ritual is not forgotten.

But the English Church remains empty save for one or two, and a tucktoo in the roof who is rude with his interruptions, and the clergyman himself, who is a Club Member. Yet whenever I have gone there he is always collecting money for Foreign Missions to gather in the heathen.

Besides the churches aforementioned we have

in Myosein several Joss Houses, two Pagodas, and a Mosque, to say nothing of wayside shrines, so it must be conceded we do our several Gods very well, and spiritually we should lack nothing.

Thank you for your sympathy over the loss of my friend. I can even yet not believe that he is indeed gone, and six months afterwards I find myself half expecting to see him seated in his office beneath the punkah, laughing at something amusing in the course of our work, that no one else would have noticed, and to hear him say:

"Nehra, I never chips, nor cracks. . . ."

In his place we now have Mr. Nigel Hill, acting. He is young for the job and I fancy has been given the chance that they may see how he manages, and certainly he will manage splendidly. He is a brilliant young man, with a brain that immediately seizes the essentials in any situation, and lets the rest go, and so he gets through things much quicker than more plodding and pedantic folk. For instance, on hearing my name, he has instantly and without hesitation made a joke about it:

"Nehra my God to Thee," said Mr. Hill. But for all this brilliance and this competence, he lacks that kindly human touch that makes all the difference when dealing with People, and not

Files. His job he knows from A to Z, but what is going on in the heart of the simple people around him, he would consider it beneath his dignity to know, and cannot even bother to guess. And because of this, they do not like him. What a contrast I find it working with him after Mr. Chelston. Mr. Hill does not care any more for Indians, or damn Wogs, than he did when first I came here, and so once more I live and work in isolation.

Last night we celebrated the Armistice here and for your amusement I must tell you something about that, since of late I seem only to have had depressing things to tell you. At the Club I met the Captain of a cargo ship lying further up the river taking in a cargo of rice.

He said, seeing it was Armistice night, wouldn't it be a good thing if we did something to celebrate it, and everyone said, "But, what can we do to celebrate it?" He said the thing would be to send up a rocket. They were forced to own they had not got such a thing in all Myosein, but the Captain said, "Don't be silly, there are always rockets on a ship in case of shipwreck."

So we all went with him, about six of us, to let off and celebrate the Armistice. It was one of the larger cargo boats on which I found myself, all very clean and well kept, and there was a Scotch Engineer so national that I could not understand one word of what he was saying, but he produced the rocket, a very formidable affair, and presently it transpired that nobody was very sure how to let it off. The Captain and the Engineer it seemed had been wrecked so little that they had got out of practice, because they had never had to fire a rocket at all before. However, after some unintelligible talk on the part of the Engineer, they lashed it to the rail and someone set a light and we all stood round breathlessly waiting, watching the stars amongst which our rocket was soon to appear.

Alas, it did not appear there. With a sudden hiss it broke, and the top half fell on to the deck and wriggled with deadly precision of a snake returning to its master, towards the Engineer, and in spite of all his efforts to avoid it it shot up his trouser leg and exploded with a loud explosion in the seat of his pants.

So we celebrated the Armistice in Myosein with full honour, but it was sad for the Engineer who was carried to Hospital on a stretcher, face downwards, and now perhaps it is a good thing that nothing he has ever said was intelligible to me.

They would have to carry him past the windows of the Sailors' Home, and no doubt the old lady looked out hungrily and made enquiries, and was disappointed to hear that it was not bad enough to mean another funeral.

XII

SINCE writing to you last much has happened and life has not been too pleasant. I left Myosein at the beginning of the Hot Weather, having at length found myself forced to apply for a transfer. Things became unpleasant after Mr. Hill took over Mr. Chelston's work, and they grew steadily more so. Mr. Hill did not like me, and was not prepared to give me a fair chance. If he had his way all Indians would be blown from the guns, beheaded, or hung in that popular gallows where the Kaiser also swings. He does not scruple to say so in my presence, and this I find increasingly depressing. At first I have told myself he will get over this prejudice. But soon I discovered that if you take that away, there is no Mr. Hill left.

I have been in many difficult and unpleasant positions because of it, for other natives, realizing the situation, have sought to use it for their own ends. And yet other natives, resenting it for me, would have retaliated in manners known to themselves, but for my stern intervention.

I have received even a secret communication from the Bazaar, offering for fifty-five rupees to rid me of this officer for ever. I have been long enough away from the East to see the funny side of this sort of thing, but also inside me is the old Adam so strong, that at the same time I almost wish that I could avail myself of the opportunity on some occasions, when I smarted more than others under his sarcasm.

One day, when we had had some very unpleasant conversation, Mr. Hill told me frankly that he hated my country and everything to do with it. Whereupon I asked him, not unreasonably I hope, why if this was the case, he had ever come to it. Whereupon he replied grimly enough:

"Because, Nehra, I, like other people, have got to live."

I did not point out to him how easily he might have died, had I so minded. Mr. Hill would not be likely to see the funny side of that joke.

This I fancy, is one of the real problems, those who come out because at an early age they hope to draw a pension, and without any friendliness for India in their heart.

I have endeavoured to exercise patience but at last the situation became too unpleasant, and I have applied for a transfer. Imagine my surprise to find myself transferred to Rangoon, which is officially a step up, and the last thing I expected, for Mr. Hill can have said little to my advantage in his reports.

I left Myosein without any regrets. It is a dirty place, beautiful only at the hour of sunset, which is brief and quickly over.

Now, for me, I am very well off. I have a house of my own, also a garden. But I fear there is to be as little inter-community life here as there was in Myosein. Indeed, judging from the number of clubs, Rangoon is Myosein on a larger scale. I find here no point of contact between the different races who work together during the hours of office. After that they retire into separate Clubs and once more the fortifications are up. Now I know once and for all that the old pleasant comradeship I enjoyed so much in England, amongst men who had taken the same sort of education as myself, can never be any more. Between me and them is a great gulf fixed. Once I did not see it, but now every year I am a little more aware of its wideness.

Sometimes upon my lonely walks, I think about these things, Lady Sahib, and I come to the conclusion that it is the small things that separate man from man, not the large ones. The hats, the habits, and the customs, more than the religious or political convictions. To some men the top hat must always be a joke, as with the Englishman, must always be the turban or the fez. The man who burns his grandmother up with fire when she dies, has nothing in common with he who exposes her upon the Towers of Silence, or he who, more enlightened, digs a hole and puts her into the mud.

Do you think that if one day the ingenious heart of man could invent a form of burial universally pleasing, or the ingenious mind of man a hat acceptable to all mankind, we could at last be friends?

Here I work daily in the Secretariat, which is a large building in the hottest shade of red brick embellished with yellow trimmings. It would be hard to find anything more ugly or less suited to a tropical climate and I am always wondering anew at the Governmental love of brick in a country so much better adapted to buildings of wood, which are also cheaper. Also safer in earthquakes. Not long ago there was an earthquake, and it has given a slant to the Roman Catholic Cathedral, which now has the appearance of attempting to bow to the Anglican

Cathedral, which remains stiff and proud and will not return the salute. At least, not until after another earthquake.

Amongst my work I have had sorting of files to do, and so have come one day across Myosein files, and in the middle of them Mr. Hill's reports on myself and my work. Imagine my surprise when I have found he had given me the most glowing recommendations, and has said many times "This officer is worthy of promotion." This in a way has touched me very much and from the astonishment of the discovery I have not yet recovered, for that certainly no Indian who disliked me very warmly, would have done for me.

I was delighted to get the snapshots of yourself and your small son. I thought perhaps you had forgotten that I once asked you for one, or considered my request presumptuous. The small David is, I think, like his Mother, though it is strange to me now to think that I have only seen you once, and that for little more than an hour, whom I feel I know so very well.

It will be very pleasant for you to return to England in the Spring, and show the small David his own beautiful country. It must be very nice to be born an English child, and so, one spring day when there is apple blossom upon the trees, to come to Cambridge and be able to say:

"This is my own."

Please give many salaams for me to London, where I have spent such happy times and more especially to that part of the Park that looks down towards the church at Lancaster Gate, over the water that has such self-satisfied ducks upon it. It is a strange thing that when in your churches I have heard them talk of heaven, I see always that part of London, looking over the water towards Lancaster Gate, and indeed, a man might do worse.

Also my salaams to the Opera Arcade, where there is a small shop containing a small man who sells the best silk handkerchiefs in the world. How many places there will be for me to visit when I return again to England.

XIII

TO-DAY I have received from you some beautiful silk handkerchiefs from the Opera Arcade shop and what am I to say to you for giving me this wonderful surprise? That you should also have remembered my little shop, and my little man, is such a very kind thing that I do not know how I am ever going to put into words my thanks for it.

How glad I was to learn that my little man still sits there, for in my heart there is always a fear that when my time comes I shall return there and find the shutters up, and the little old man flown away to that heaven where good haberdashers go. Since last I saw him he must be very much older, although he then seemed so old that no further changes could possibly take place.

There are as usual changes to report to you, for here it is not as peaceful as the Opera Arcade where a man can sit and continue to look the same for one hundred years. I am still in Rangoon, working in the Courts, and find it interesting, if at times disheartening. Theories when put into practice, work out so very differently to what it is hoped and intended, and often one has to see the spirit of Justice travestied to keep the letter. I am often disheartened in these days with the disheartenment of the mouse who works his small wheel all day long in the heat, and discovers in the end he is no further than when he started. I do not see that we approach any better understanding than when I came out first, so many years ago. All we do is amass Files, and more Files.

Since writing to you last I have married. She is a nice girl, well-known to my family, and has for some time been chosen for me by them. She will no doubt bear me many sons, and keep my house in order. With us marriage is not the same as with you. Our women are for the most part un-educated and there is, for those of us accustomed to the ways of the West, no companionship to be had with them. For a little while I tried, kindly, to make her interested in the things that interest me, but soon see it is no good. There are many things I envy in the West, and that a man in marrying should find also a companion and a friend with whom he can discuss matters of interest to him, is perhaps the greatest of them. It would be a splendid thing to have a wife with whom one could have more in common than just the going to bed and having children. But for us it is as yet not to be. Only here and there are our women emancipated, and then for them the state is such a new one that they are apt to lose their heads and make a great deal of trouble and noise.

Already at nineteen, Mala is a Matron. She thinks only of things to do with the house. She becomes stout. I have endeavoured for a time to make her ride horseback, and play golf, but it was asking too much of one who wishes only to sit upon the housetop, waiting for her Lord and Master to return.

We remain still in the same house. The British Community, the Indian Community, the Chinese Community, they flourish and increase, but between them there are no points of contact, and any meetings that take place are always in a state of armed neutrality. The fortifications for a moment are down, but one word, and up they will go again, and all the time we are waiting for that word.

For many years it has been the custom of the English people to make the Burman remove his shoes and kneel when he enters the august presence. Now the Burman is of a sudden retaliating, and insists that the Englishman shall also remove his shoes if he wishes to enter their Pagodas. Over the entrance of each Pagoda a new notice hangs:

"No Footwearing or Umbrellering."

To umbreller, you must understand, is to carry in the hand this instrument, and use it for pointing out the various kinds of carving on the shrines, and the Burman has of a sudden said to himself, "Since I must kneel in the presence of my employer and go barefoot, booted and umbrellering shall he not come here."

Over this there is much out-cry and I have been told that it is a damned piece of impertinence, and find myself often wondering why it is that your countryman—so kind and so humorous in his own land—should inevitably become so pompous and so inhuman in this. Perhaps it is the heat that does it.

Mr. Nigel Hill came through Rangoon last week. I met him in the Club and would have liked to speak to him and congratulate him upon his new post, but he so patently did not see me, and did not wish to see me, that my courage failed me.

In India there is much upheaval and unrest, and my letters bring me no good tidings. What is to be the end of it all, I do not know. There is now a large and growing faction who would say to the Government "Clear out". But what they suggest putting into its place is not clear. My own people are in the main both foolish and extravagant, and very often dishonest, as we find only too frequently in those departments where they have at present a free hand. They have much to learn, but I cannot see they will learn it in any good heart until there is friendship between them and their masters.

I was very sorry to hear that you would come to India no more, though I knew that the Colonel Sahib's time must soon be up. This puts an end for ever to my hope that one day I shall get a transfer and find to my delight it is to some place where I can come at last and pay my respects to you, and thank you for many great kindnesses. Those first days of adjustment when I returned to the East and had to find my place there were not pleasant ones for me, and your friendship and interest I now know meant a great deal more to me than I realized at the time, and went a long way to helping me not to lose heart entirely.

However, one day I shall certainly take a holiday and come to England. It is a dream I often allow myself, and much look forward to making one day come true.

XIV

My small son was born last week, and is to be called Arvind, after me. When he is a little less ugly I shall send you a snapshot of him. Mala is up and around the house again. To her, having children it is nothing.

The child is well and strong, and gives no trouble. I spend much time admiring him. When all is said and done, it is the primal joys that are the most intense. He who conquers a country or rises to great prominence and honour gets out of it not one pleasure more than he who, sitting in the sunshine, watches his firstborn's efforts to remove a finger, or suck a toe.

XV

CHRISTMAS is not legitimately any feast of mine
save that it is the feast of children, and being
myself a Father my heart must be soft towards
all children. For this reason it is rapidly becoming a feast of mine. I can now rely upon
a letter from you at that season, with your news.
I find it difficult to believe that this large boy
in the snapshot is indeed David. Time falls away
so fast one does not realize that it is going.

I remain in Rangoon, but shall shortly be
promoted. I am now a full-fledged Judge of the
High Court. My next move will no doubt be
India and I shall be glad to get back there,
for the news we get is far from good. What is to
come of all this agitation for Home Rule, I cannot
make out.

Here in Burma there is also a certain unrest,
but it is not very much as yet. The sun
shines, there is a Religious Festival to keep,
someone makes a large tiger and plays music
inside him, and the Burman forgets. Indeed
at heart he is no Politician, and has no aspira-

tions beyond a full stomach. In my opinion at the bottom of all Political aspirations it boils down to that. It is only when a people becomes poverty-stricken that it grows discontented and seeks to better its ways with quack medicines.

I have now four children. Arvind, my first-born, is a strong boy of seven. Your David must now be nine. There are two other sons and a daughter. Mala has indeed done her duty and becomes now very stout. It is a pity but it cannot be helped. At twenty-seven she is quite the old lady. Our women fade quickly, and they do not care. To grow old and stout with child-bearing, it is an honourable thing, and one that nobody fears. As yet there are no beauty parlours in our midst, save those dark arts our old women impart to the Brides.

Rangoon is very changed. The streets are now thronged with motor cars, and there are still two more Clubs building. Everybody appears to be immensely rich, and indeed we draw here princely pay. It is pleasant, but always in my secret heart I wonder, is it wise? Because at the back of it all, there sits always the small man in the jungle, the little man with two or three rice fields, and he it is who is taxed to

pay all this money and only as long as he is contented and satisfied can there be any quiet in the
land. Already travelling in the Districts, I have
heard murmurs.

There has come amongst us also, since the
War, a new kind of official. He is not the type
of man the East got years ago, but a new kind
of whom I would say that he was born tired.
And he has come out East, like Mr. Nigel Hill,
not from any sense of vocation such as fired the
young men in the days when Mr. Kipling wrote
his poems, but because he must live, and wishes
as soon as possible to draw a pension. And always
he hates the damn country.

At first I treated it lightly thinking it was a
pose like the young man at Cambridge who said
"I never do any work", and then was always
swotting behind closed doors when he pretended
to sleep. Of late I come -to the conclusion this
is not so. For many things are troublesome here
now, and nothing is done. Only we continue to
do exactly what was laid down yesterday.
Nothing new is allowed under the sun, even
when the old is obviously worn threadbare, and
bad. From time to time I have spoken to you
about taxes. I shall now quote you an instance.
There is in the Districts much real poverty

because of the fall in the price of rice. Rice, which the cultivator now sells at from sixty to seventy rupees one hundred baskets, he at one time got over one hundred rupees for. But the tax remains the same as when he got one hundred rupees. We are rapidly approaching a state of things when the profit upon the rice is nothing, and still he has the tax to pay.

Perhaps you will ask why the tax cannot fall automatically with the price of the rice? Because, Lady Sahib, the cost of Government administration does not fall, it grows every year heavier. It is a bad thing for a country when the small man in the jungle murmurs and grows discontented.

Meanwhile, Government salaries continue large, much larger than the same men could ever hope to get had they remained in England. I myself receive a salary that is ridiculously high. It is pleasant and I enjoy it, but in my heart alone I doubt if it is wise. And all around us, red brick buildings are springing up, the realization of this or that high-flown scheme, often not too well thought out.

I who admire and love England so much, often feel to-day that she is like one who has taken bad advice and is for a moment deserting her better judgments, for profligate ways. Certainly the Western Administration of to-day is too expensive, and too complicated for the Eastern nations, and that is at the root of all the troubles realized and brewing. When it is written of any country, "The people cried out under the burden of the taxes" then that chapter is to be a sad one.

One sees a repercussion of all this in the Courts where there are many crimes from poverty, and much violence in the District, resisting tax collections, but so far it is on a small scale, little. The sun shines and the Burman forgets.

Do I offend you, Lady Sahib, in writing to you like this? I hope not. In my present position there is not a soul to whom I can speak out and frankly, for whatever my private convictions may be, officially I must uphold the system entirely and without reservation. No one realizes more than I the necessity for absolute loyalty on the part of Government Servants in these days, and how any move that is made must be made by the body as a whole, not here one and there one.

To-night I shall dine with a brother Judge in his beautiful house out beside the Lakes.

From time to time I am now asked to dine in the British Community but always I see in the eyes of my Hostess that old terror lest I shall not behave properly at table. We shall have eight courses to eat, and many expensive drinks, and all the talk will be of how hard up everyone is and what difficult times these are. There will be only elderly English ladies from the Hospital and Schools present, for the difficulties of these mixed dinner parties is an acute one, and no one appreciates it now more than myself.

For this, Lady Sahib, is the problem stripped of all its frills and varnish. I am an Indian, and have growing sons, and if my sons mix with your daughters, perhaps they will fall in love with one another. The colour problem is the sex problem, the problem of the outcast and half-breed. However much we may like one another, we do not wish our children to inter-marry. All our inhibitions and our precautions and our fortifications against each other's communities are because of this one great and not-alluded-to fact. To the pure bred, the half-breed must always be a disaster. Could one ever overcome that instinctive feeling? Would it be desirable if one did?

In America I am told they are evolving a super-man from all the nations under the sun. I would prefer to see him for myself, before passing any opinion on this result of the melting pot.

As I grow older, I think there is no colour problem, but this one of sex, just as there are no National Problems, only problems of Finance. A country has vested interests in another country, and like Pharaoh of old, when they struggle for freedom, she will not let them go. There is no new plot under the sun, Lady Sahib. Only the same old story told over and over again, with perhaps some new scenery here and there for politeness' sake.

But Nations, like people, dislike hard facts. They prefer to put a small and elegant petticoat on the naked truth. And so vested interests are called moral obligations because we feel better about it that way. So we break people's heads, lest they should break each other's.

XVI

I HAVE lost a small son. So much has this hurt me that I must sit down now to talk to you about it before I can go back to my work of every day. Only yesterday he was so well and strong, and such a healthy chap, this small boy I have called Dravid, perhaps a little for the sake of your David.

With his brothers he went bathing in the Big Lakes. It was not until they swam in again that they missed him and indeed he must have sunk without any sound, as he followed them towards the shore. All night I spent rowing about, looking for him, calling him. To-day at dawn they found his body entangled in some weeds.

To lose a son, it is in part to die oneself. A part of me that might have achieved immortality, is no more, and to-day I feel as if life held nothing more for me, and my sorrow is too great to bear. Nor does it help me to know that in time I shall forget this small boy who has climbed on my knee and lain against my heart, as others forget.

After my son is buried, I go down into the District on an Enquiry Commission into all the trouble over the taxes. Perhaps, when the poverty and hardships of the country people are brought to light, the Government will reduce somehow its heavy expenses, and be content with a quieter way of living, and ways more suited to this country.

I will write you more fully of this later on. At the moment my heart is too heavy.

XVII

YOUR letter about the death of my small boy brought me great comfort. It was a sad and bitter time, and already in the prime of life I know what it is to feel hopeless and old.

I have been much interested in your comments on what I have told you about things out here, and it is interesting that you should have come to much the same conclusions yourself, from your reading of contemporary events. In England also you say the same state of affairs approaches, and that the Government requires one-third of the Public Income. Worse than out here. I have read with much interest of this Dole, and cannot see but that in the end it must be a bad thing. It is too much like the case of the poor relation. Whilst money is coming from the rich man in another country, he is not going to bestir himself. Why should he?

Our visit to the District came to nothing. We saw many hardships and much poverty and report duly, but the Government have replied that no remittance of taxation is possible, and in this country where many poor country people are practically starving, the building of a large and palatial University now goes on. Also the making and widening of many roads for motor-cars. To the onlooker this must seem a little topsy-turvy, and into my mind come the words of your great teacher, the Christ, who said that mankind would in the end be destroyed by his own inventions.

To that unhappy end I often think we are well on the way.

In India we have a new Prophet, this Mr. Gandhi. I know little of him save that my family in India write that he is a sincere man and believes implicitly in his own heart that he is acting for the good of his country. The mistakes of the really sincere do so much more harm than the follies of the mischievous and the wilful, that I am a little anxious for Mr. Gandhi. His ideals are about as unattainable as those with which I left Cambridge. I, also, Lady Sahib, was going to make a new heaven and a new earth, and bring about a better understanding between black men and white men, and it all seemed so very easy.

Gandhi, I see, preaches that everyone must do without foreign goods and wear only the native manufactured khadda. So for interest's sake I sat down and worked this out the other night, only to discover there would be something like three inches of khadda per head of the population, and since even the loin cloth of my people requires more than this, lo, another distant Utopia!

Do you see that this Mr. Nigel Hill about whom I have at one time written you so much and so passionately, is now Chief Secretary of the Upper Provinces? There is a young man of real ability, which from the beginning I have been able to recognize through all more personal feelings, although indeed for his sake my pride has often smarted very much.

I would like to meet him again, now that we are both so much older and wiser, and I have lost most of my dreams, and know my place, and he, perhaps, has outgrown some of his prejudices. I feel in my heart there must be between us some point of contact, if only we can find it, and always I am interested in this man and feel in some strange manner bound up with him.

Never can I quite forget that although he disliked me personally, he gave me a glowing recommendation which has helped me on a good deal in my career. I myself would have had difficulty to do a thing like that.

XVIII

I HEAR only this morning that I am to be transferred, first for a spell of short duty to Shillong, and then to Calcutta where I am likely to be for some little time.

I do not at all know this side of India very well, nor have I ever been up to any Hill Station, so this will be an adventure for me. Mala, poor girl, is appalled at the prospect, and all these journeyings. Our women do not move with the times, or at best only slowly, slowly, and still to Mala the old things are the best. The household Gods, the sacrifices, the observing of unenlightened ritual—to my wife these are still the things that matter, and beyond them she does not care to look.

Never has she quite forgiven me, because I have made her uncover her face, and live a natural life, going about with me to a certain extent. For the Mother of Mala entered her husband's house at the time of her marriage and did not leave it again until her death, and to Mala this is the right and proper behaviour for modest women, and often she weeps and tells me I have made her outcast because in our household we no longer observe certain rules, and certain customs. Then I must go shopping and get her a bright sari, and for a little while Mala's tears are stopped.

It takes three generations, Lady Sahib, before the old voices no longer call. Three generations is a long time. No wonder our masters grow a little impatient with us! In my own home when I was a child, we made punctual and often bloody sacrifices to the domestic Gods, and listened to the voices of the Old Women, who would not let us put aside one jot of that ritual. My own Mother was little more than a slave to her Mother-in-law, who ruled us all with a rod of iron. The Indian *Dhai*[1] has brought myself and my brothers into the world, with varying degrees of success in conditions too filthy to dwell upon.

And yet what trouble have I had with Mala my wife, to persuade her into the Hospital for attention? It is to the *Dhai* and her black arts Mala, left to herself, would turn, just as, were I to die, I am sure she would do her best, somehow or other to burn herself upon some convenient bonfire.

[1]Midwife

[84]

Three generations it takes, of which Mala is the first, and I am only the second. For my own Father, after prolonged travelling in the West, discontinued many practices that had been common to us, opened the large windows of our house, letting some sunshine in, and spoke often to us, his sons, of the more enlightened means of sanitation and medicine, and of the evil some of our customs have caused amongst us. He caused also my sisters to uncover their faces.

What outcry there was, too. What talk and scandal amongst the old women because my Father has refused to sanction the burning up of my Uncle's widow, and has settled a portion upon her and treated her kindly.

One step away from these old customs stand I—and do not care for them, Lady Sahib. But because they were my childhood, they are in my blood. I could find it easily in my heart to covenant for the removal of my enemy for a cash payment! The dark rites of some of our sacrifices—to me they still have some appeal. In my own heart I must still sometimes bow to the Priestess of Ancient Custom.

But my son—look—he is the third generation, and to him it all means nothing. He has not seen the child bride weeping about his home, he has never sacrificed to Kali. To him, educated mainly in the West, free and innocent intercourse between men and women will not be unthinkable.

I have hopes for my son and his generation. They do not hear, as we hear them, the calling of drums in the village, or the overpowering threats from the Temple.

For us, the older men, I do not think there is much hope to see the light. Our old men, your old men, they are all hemmed around with prejudices, and if we cannot forget the backyard sacrificings of goats, and the blood poured out—neither can your old men forget the banner that flew upon the highest walls at Lucknow — and the unsalubrious cellar in Calcutta.

But for your son, Lady Sahib, and my son—perhaps friends, perhaps working side by side, what do you think?

XIX

INDEED, in India also are some very beautiful and pleasant places, and once arrived here how very nice it is to see green rolling downland, and many pine trees with their resinous smell. Here are the roads all pink, and hedged about with hydrangea hedges all in flower, a soft blue colour not unlike the wistaria I remember about the colleges in my beloved Cambridge.

But the getting here! Indeed with a wife and family, many servants and cooking pots, it was no joke. Because one must mount by a controlled road, upon which it is possible to go up only between the hours of eleven and one—and after that, one must stand still unless one has planned capably, and allow for the traffic which may only go down. I knowing but little of this part of the world, schemed unwisely, therefore were we stuck many hours, with my poor wife waiting for the tiger to emerge from the jungle and devour her, or the elephant to trample our caravan into the earth.

None of these disasters occurred, mercifully.

Indeed one cannot help seeing they are wise to so control the road, because of many places where for two motor cars to pass, it is not possible. Four thousand feet below, the river flows beyond a stiff wall of jungle, amongst which there are many sharp rocks. It is beautiful indeed, but I am rather prevented from admiring it because my stomach rebels shortly against the swing of the car, and one and all we become sea-sick.

So we shall not in a hurry forget our coming to Shillong.

However, now that we are here it is very pleasant, and even Mala has to own it. We have a nice wooden house with its own garden, in excellent order, because recently vacated by a European Commissioner.

There is up here one British Regiment, and several Civil Servants, besides the large Hospital some way out of the town. I believe that I am eligible for the European Club, but I do not think I shall go to it, since to go there only rubs in that of which I am already well aware, and now in my old age I become rather shy!

The hill natives are a short, stout and friendly people, who one and all salute the passer-by with *"Gubalay, gubalay . . ."* The general idea amongst English people up here, I find, is that it is an echo of the better known cry of "Baksheesh!" This is not the case, for all these short little men, these sturdy women and quaint flat-faced children with their extremely dirty clothes have to say to the stranger, is just "God bless you . . ." That is all.

I do not function here in Shillong itself, but go out on District work, and it is very interesting though perhaps a little depressing, bringing still more clearly to mind the complexity of the problem with which we endeavour to deal. Amongst the hill people, human sacrifice is still practised on the sly, and purely from the highest motives, and one of my chief duties here is to endeavour to put a stop to this sordid business.

But I shall tell you something more about that later on, when I have made my tour.

XX

Now I can tell you a little more of some of my work up here, which may perhaps be of interest to you. And first and most formidable of all, behold our local Snake.

He dwells in a cleft up here on the mountain side, in a large fissure that was caused by an earthquake. For I must tell you, this part of the world is very prone to earthquakes, and for this reason, very sensibly no brick building must be of more than three feet high, after that your edifice must all be composed of wood, or of plaster and lathes, so that he who gets fallen upon by his house in an earthquake, is not fallen upon too much.

Now you and I may have our private ideas as to the causes of these earthquakes, but that makes no difference to the small unlettered man in the country about here, Lady Sahib. Because, you see, he knows. And what he knows is that the earthquakes come because the Snake has been allowed to get angry, and then through the earth he goes, and confides his troubles to the spirits that sit within the earth, and then the spirits get angry as well, and then, *pouff*, down come all our houses about our heads.

The small man in the village *knows* this, just as he knows that anything we may say to him to the contrary proves only our ignorance, or that we have some private axe to grind. Do not ever suppose, Lady Sahib, that it is by its Rulers and more enlightened men a country is really governed. It is by the small men in the villages—who *know*.

Another thing the small man knows is just how to placate this angry Snake, and the way it is done is as follows. Once yearly you must make chupattis mixed with the best of flour and ghee, and all welded together with human blood. It is useless trying to palm off goat's blood upon this very intelligent Snake. He knows what he wants.

And the small man in the village is going to see he gets it, and hence comes much trouble for me, who am a servant of the Government whose face is turned against human sacrifice unless done by four wheels in a City street to the Goddess of Speed!

I have accommodated myself in the Rest House as usual, using the open space in front of the bungalow as my Court. From far and near the villagers have come, some on foot, some riding their tats, some in carts that proclaim their coming from afar. On the faces of many I see plainly enough a positive disgust that it is a black man like themselves who has come to attend to their grievances. For this is one of the paradoxes out here . . . The Indian is all for Home Rule—but if he has a Law-Suit, he prefers it to come before the English Judge—and if he has a disease, and is rich enough to afford it—he will usually go to the English Doctor.

With me has come the Deputy Commissioner of these parts, an elderly Bengali gentleman with much stomach in front, and a great dislike for exerting himself, and I do not think he has much conception of a law higher than personal ambition, or clan advantage. In his District I cannot help but notice that all executive posts within his gift are held by his relations, who no doubt paid a cash bonus on assuming them.

So, out there in this open space we try our cases. This man has put a spell upon his neighbour's cow. This man has forcibly removed a wife from her tent and children, for his own use. I have also before me two murderers, pleading, of course, Not Guilty, since in this country no one would dream of pleading anything else. Each of them has a great multiplicity of witnesses, and I know they are lying, and they know that I, being one of themselves, am well aware that they are lying. That is partly why they do not like it when they perceive it is not a white man who is come to judgment!

So through three days we labour as best may be, and so we come again to our Snake. Last week, punctual as usual to the very day the body of an Indian has been found, badly and unpleasantly mutilated, close behind the entrance to the dwelling place of this sacred Reptile.

Yearly this same affair occurs. Yearly there appears to be no clue whatever to who is responsible for it, and seated in this house at evening, I have discussed this matter at some length with my Bengali official, and the local Policeman, who is a Gurkha.

They have, it appears, no knowledge at all of who is at the bottom of all this.

"But surely," I point out, "knowing that this thing takes place yearly, it would be possible to keep watch, and take some steps of prevention? You have here a Headman who would surely help you?"

The Policeman, and my Colleague look both furtive and a little guilty. It is, they say, very difficult, because the people are an ignorant and superstitious people, and to tamper with their religious beliefs is very dangerous.

"But you are here, paid by the Government, to stop these unenlightened and savage practices," I have pointed out to my Bengali friend. Yes, yes, he says. That is so. Whilst the Gurkha Policeman is present, he is all on my side, protesting windily that something must be done before another year is out.

No sooner has the Policeman departed, than he becomes suddenly confidential. His official air dropping from him, my Bengali colleague now talks to me as from man to man.

"It is all very well, Nehra. You know how things are. . . . This is a matter in which I cannot interfere. This is a matter of religious observance. . . ."

In his eye I can see quite plainly now the truth, which is that he also, though a Government Official, is of the opinion this Snake must at all costs be placated—and of what matter is the death of one unimportant man, compared with the wiping out of many villages through earthquake and upheaval?

You see, Lady Sahib? He is the first generation attempting to become civilized. He cannot quite break away. And in my own heart I know that I, the second generation, one step farther on towards the light of saner ways—were I stationed up here in the hills alone with the wild people who hold these beliefs, could very easily become also of his mind! Though I have no wish to arise and join in an orgy of human sacrifice, to me the drums still call. They do not make me wish to follow, but I can hear them.

Unless you were so much my good friend, and able to take the worst along with the best, as good friends must, I would not dare to tell you this. Amongst my Official Superiors I also would stroke the chin, even as my Bengali gentleman does, and fold my hands on my stomach, and say:

"Yes, yes. . . . This is a very superstitious and unenlightened people. We must certainly deal with the matter forthwith."

XXI

IT has been so long since I hear anything from you that I am become afraid that something may have happened to you, and perhaps out of my life one of its greatest pleasures has gone for ever, and that I found a very depressing thought.

This morning it was comfortably dispelled, for here is your letter, telling me of long disasters with measles and mumps, and I am so relieved it is nothing but that. Could you perhaps in some future letter tell me what it is, the mump? I cannot find it in my dictionary, and do not seem ever to have come across it.

How glad I am to hear young David is after all no worse for his adventures of the body, as I trust you are no worse for yours of the spirit. The anxieties of parents for their children, what an unpleasant experience. But regarding them also no doubt you have your philosophy.

I wrote last I think from Shillong, where I enjoyed my short spell of duty very much, and escaped at last quite unscathed by earthquake in spite of lack of co-operation with Sacred Snake.

Up there I felt rather like Gulliver when he was upon that floating island of his, for indeed we seemed at all times to have little connexion of any sort with the Plains, and orders issued there arrived like a very distant echo, often long after any chance of carrying them out had disappeared. Indeed, in these out of the way places, much lies in the hands of the man on the spot, and all is well as long as he has the initiative necessary.

I remember my dear friend Mr. Chelston telling me of an English soldier in charge of outpost on the frontier, who after much trouble with one village, wired to headquarters for permission to blow up said village.

Many delays took place over his wire, from storms, mishaps, and red tape, and it was ten days before the reply came:

"On no account blow up village."

To which the reply was then sent:

"Blew up village three days ago."

And since the blowing up had been an entirely successful one, nothing more was heard of it by the man on the spot. No doubt if anything had gone wrong, much would have been heard, but, said Mr. Chelston to me, a man who is a man will take that chance. He will not chip or crack—but what he smashes, he will smash utterly!

The older I grow the more often do I find myself building my conduct on scraps of wisdom I gathered as a young man from this friend, now such a long time dead. I do not think it is only the evil that men do lives after them, Lady Sahib.

But to tell you something more of our present circumstances. Here we are, in Calcutta, penned meantime in a Flat until there is a house available for us. My family is not a Flat-sized family and so we are not too comfortable. I hope later to get out somewhere in the Ballygunge direction, to a house with a garden or at least the old-fashioned flat roof on which my many children may play.

Here in Calcutta is a large Indian Community, of course, so we can lead quite a large social life of our own. The first ceremony to which I have been gave me a very heavy heart. It is the marriage of a cousin of my own who has still observed all the old caste rules and so forth, and his Bride, she is a small girl of ten years old.

Picture that, Lady Sahib. At the age of ten, when in Cambridge little girls are laughing a great deal and rolling hoops here and there, and pushing their dolls in perambulators beside pleasant Nurses and companions—to have to become married to a man of my age, and one who has had already three wives before.

I have not seen this little Bride. I am a man, and so she cannot look upon my face. But the knowledge of her presence in the Zenana there in my cousin's house, about to come under the thrall of her Mother-in-law, and into the hands of the old women, has turned me very heavy.

My cousin was married first at the age of thirteen. His wife of that time was eight. What can any boy make of life, when taken up so early with the matters of the body? It is a shame amongst us. Bringing to the living with his wife all the immoderate zeal of the young with a new hobby, already at twenty-five he was an old man.

And now, behind the curtains, there is that little girl, brought up to think of her husband as a God who can do no wrong.

Largely have I spoken against these things in my own family, with the result that I am threatened by many Pundits with damnation, not only in this, but in various coming reincarnations.

I am not a very learned man, but I will take the risk. From the beginning I have striven to turn the minds of my sons from these matters, hampered a little by my wife, who, woman-like, considers that which always has been, is best. Besides, she is afraid of what the old women will say.

XXII

I HAVE lost a small daughter very sadly and in a way that could have been prevented, and meantime my heart is very sore. My wife, Mala, has become a follower of great immoderation of Mr. Gandhi, and since Mr. Gandhi has written that "European Doctors are the worst of all, because they violate our religious instincts and mix their medicines with the fats of forbidden animals—and that to study European medicine is to deepen our slavery", behold Mala will have nothing to do with the Hospital and when my small daughter fell ill, it was to the Ayervedic doctor she looked for help.

Many there are out here who uphold our Ayervedic school of medicine, even amongst the intelligent and I do not for a moment doubt myself that in amongst all that ancient learning there is collected some understanding of drugs. When it is nothing of any account, the small stomach ache, the pain in the kidneys, I let Mala have her way. This a man does, for peace at home. But when my small daughter is taken ill and after physicings becomes no better, I have gone to the Doctor I happen to have met from time to time, up at the Hospital, one Major Shawn, and I lay before him my case and mention as best may be, the symptoms.

He tells me certainly it is appendicitis my child suffers from, and advises me to bring her to him.

"Operated on at once, and in time, there is no danger, Nehra . . ." he told me, and he patted me very kindly on the back, since he also is a Father and can understand what I am feeling.

How many hours have I talked with Mala? I cannot remember, and now I am too tired to consider it any more. She has summoned also to her aid her Mother, of whom I am soon heartily tired. Between them they overpersuade me against my own better judgment to leave the child yet one more day.

"Take her to the Hospital and they will cut her open with knives and kill her."

So we continue yet a little while, treating my child with this system in which there is nothing approaching definite understanding of physical problems, and a great deal of voodoo and dealings with evil spirits. And by midnight it is obvious that my child is so ill she must presently die, and even Mala grew a little frightened, and came to me saying perhaps after all we had better take her to the English Major Sahib.

In the middle of the night we go. Major Shawn very kindly rises from his bed and at two in the morning they operate on my child. But before they do so, Major Shawn told me it was now a very grave case, having been left too long.

"If you had brought the child to me at once, it would have been easy," he told me.

Now she is dead, and my house is full of lamentations and the upbraiding of women's voices, who tell me I have murdered my child. "What did the Mahatama say?" Mala had demanded of me, many times, weeping, weeping. How can I reason with them, who are as yet little children in understanding? I must sit still and have patience. What patience I can!

So you can imagine my bitterness when I see in the papers that Mr. Gandhi himself has now had appendicitis, and casting from him this Ayervedic physician of his, has taken himself forthwith to the Indian Medical Service surgeon, and has been operated upon with success, and nursed by hygienic methods and an English nursing Sister—back to that health which through him my small girl was denied!

Out here there are too many voices crying in the wilderness, Lady Sahib, and all of them crying the wrong thing.

This I have pointed out to Mala and that old woman her mother, who remains most tediously with us. What do they say?

They say it is not true. That an enemy spreads this report. That it is evil propaganda of the Sircar.

For myself, there is only this comfort. It would have been more disastrous had it been the death of a son.

XXIII

MUCH work, Lady Sahib, and nothing I can feel would be of great interest to tell you about. We have little plots of sedition, and a few bombs. A great deal of talk and not very much action. To-day from my verandah I see almost the whole of my neighbours are packing up and leaving.

Fearful of the Plague, a real menace out here, I make enquiries, to find that the Chinaman at the end of the street has recently insured his house against fire. . . .

"And what," say my neighbours one and all, "can that mean but one thing? Therefore come with us to safety."

I shall remain where I am. Firstly because my house is, after all, of stone, and so unlikely to go up, even if my Chinese neighbour should shortly wish to realize his investments.

It was pleasant to hear such good news of you, and that David has settled down comfortably in his little school after some homesickness. My children, also, grow. Arvind, my first born, is a little spoilt by his mother, which I at all times endeavour to counteract. I fancy perhaps he has some brains in his head.

With the season of the custard apple came as usual, the cholera, and I have had some difficulty persuading Mala that it is a better thing to pay attention to the cleanliness of the kitchens and the boiling of all drinking water, than the propitiation of angry spirits and offended Gods with offerings of goats' blood.

For this she waits daily to see me felled by a thunder-bolt, but to date I survive and remain in reasonable health.

Sometimes here at this function or that, I come across men who were up at St. John's with me years ago, and one and all they do not remember me. Is it not disappointing to have so little bond with one's spiritual home? The Doctor of whom I spoke to you, Major Shawn, has however been very kind indeed, and now has complete charge of the insides of all my children. From time to time I go to his house. Since all his family are at home, this is easy. Talking with him of many things that interest us both, and of our poor India now staggering so drunkenly towards—we hope—a better understanding of her own problems, almost there are times I can forget my face is a black one, and his white. In a certain kindly tolerance and breadth of humanity, this man reminds me a little of Mr. Chelston.

Here and there in a life time, a few people stand out either for agreeableness, or for disagreeableness, amongst all other people, and are, I suppose, the ones who really matter.

No one who has not worked in the Courts out here can conceive the difficulties under which we labour. In the English Courts I have visited, I noticed there was always a reasonable chance that a man on oath would speak at least part of the truth. Here, to expect such a thing is indeed a forlorn hope. So one dredges amongst a multitude of hired witnesses and erroneous statements, for one little grain of likelihood.

Recently I have sat for a long time upon the case of one Chinaman who is running out here a very flourishing drug traffic. No sooner has it become evident to him that his game is up, and the elaborate erection of lies and mis-statements about to tumble about his ears, than this man appears at my private house in the evening hours (being out on Bail). He is a person of some culture, widely travelled, and he came to me well dressed in rich clothing, driven in a yellow car of an extravagant kind. For a long time we sit paying mutual compliments, whilst I wonder what is at the back of it all and have my deep suspicions. At last without much beating up of the bush, he arrives at the point.

"Now, Mr. Nehra. How much?"

So I say to him as kindly as can be, "I hope you are not endeavouring offer me a bribe, because you must understand I cannot take it, and in itself this is a very grave offence against law."

"Perhaps ten thousand rupees?" says he, quietly.

I tell him he is wasting his time.

"Fifteen thousand rupees?"

So we continue, with ever growing astonishment on his behalf that I, an Indian, have not my price, to the sum of fifty thousand rupees. Consider all that money to be made by a comparatively poor man, just for a little matter of adjusting his point of view! Indeed, certainly out here it is often done, which explains the magnificent motor cars of many men on small salaries.

So presently he departs, not impressed by my restraint. Only amazed that any man who is such a fool can have achieved the standing I have in the community.

Of the same opinion also is the Mother of Mala, who has listened at the door.

Thorny is the path of those who endeavour to introduce foreign standards into the home circle!

XXIV

SINCE there is no peace for the wicked, I was not as long as expected for Calcutta, but suddenly torn away because of an unexpected assassination, to duty in Bombay, and here we all are, settled into our new house in some splendour, on Malabar Hill. It is good to be back again in my own part of the world, for of all the hats and customs the ingenious brain of man can invent, those to which he is accustomed must always seem the most comfortable.

I have just received your long and interesting letter. Also the parcel of books, which was a real kindness, since nowadays, even when I have the leisure to go book buying, I hardly know which to purchase so that I may keep up with that other side of the world.

Your small David, no longer small, has departed for his Public School! This is an amazement, for only yesterday it seems I heard of his arrival, quite new. I was much interested in all you tell me of the English Public Schools of to-day. I remember that Mr. Chelston often discussed with me this same matter, and told me that at Eton, where he was, to have as much as one button upon the shirt that was unlike every other button on everybody else's shirt, was considered a terrible thing. Surely this would tend to turn out the type of young man too ready to go with any crowd, anywhere? I notice in the young Englishman of to-day who come out to us here, a lot of this. Because something was done for fifty years—it cannot be improved upon and so much goes on being done for ever. Amongst them I see to-day few Mr. Chelstons, who seeing clearly a thing has got to be done, went quietly and did it, not wondering whether or no it would jeopardise his chance of a Pension!

David's school, you say, is of a newer kind in which a boy is encouraged to develop his own ideas if he has got any. This surely must be to the good. Too much guidance is as harmful to the young as insufficient discipline.

You are also inclined to lay blame for much that happens out here on Gandhi. My own personal experience of the results of his muddled thinking, have been sad and tragic ones. Yet from my heart I believe him to be no adventurer out for personal advantage and advertisement.

He is a deeply sincere man, who sees himself as a voice crying in the wilderness. The cry indeed comes from the heart. It is our national misfortune that it is the wrong cry.

I hold no brief for him. He has now stirred up forces he himself cannot control, and so we are all nicely inside the fish kettle. The situation is now out of his hands and he cannot get it back again.

But here was, I think, some zeal and some ability that rightly used might have been for good. Much of the trouble out here to-day comes from the speeches of your Politicians at home, which seem to encourage and cheer onwards those very movements the Government, on the other hand, strives to repress. Never a word is said by your local Firebrands, remember, that does not find a corner in every vernacular paper such as is read by the small man sitting round the tank in the village, or read aloud to him, with comments interspersed, by the village reader.

So they see first Gandhi is put in prison. And then he is let out again. Now he is extolled. Now it is down with him once more. Behind it all there may be some consecutive policy, but the small man beside the tank in the village cannot understand what it is. He sees confusion, and like the Irishman, gets an itch to join in.

I am weary of politics, and much distressed at the talk that now goes on in my own home. For John comes back from the Government School puffed up with every kind of wild talk, and somewhat to my dismay I find he gets a great deal of it from his Masters. Men in Government employ, mark you. Might they not take a little more trouble in the engaging of the men who are to teach our sons?

At the University where Arvind now works, is one Irishman who has on his lips the grand battle cry of "Ireland for Ever," hates the English, and makes no secret of saying to these young men that they should shake off the British yoke even as Ireland is now shaking it off.

At the age of sixteen, a high spirited boy is ready to shake off anything for the fun of the shaking.

I am now wishing very much that I had sent Arvind away from all this talk and wild nonsense, back to Cambridge, where perhaps he would have learnt a little wisdom and tolerance as well as clearer thinking. This restless atmosphere, it is not the thing for a young boy, especially one who from his more reasonable and hygienic up-bringing has much more energy and high spirits than so many of his companions. My second son, John, I shall certainly send. I shall try to bring him over myself, and hope that perhaps if I can do so, I shall be fortunate enough to meet you again, and to renew an acquaintance that is now getting quite hoary headed, although we have met in the flesh only once.

Alas, I am half afraid you would not now recognise that dark young man of slender build who stood alone beside a doorway so long ago. Indeed, I am twice the man I was, as the saying goes. And that in spite of much hard work.

Our jails are full, our Courts are working over-time over this ridiculous business of non-co-operation which will get us nowhere but into the Ditch. Already we have more prisoners than cells and sometimes have to double them up. From prisoners doubled up together no good thing comes, Lady Sahib. In many cases, those who deserve some punishment, we have to let go scot free, because we have nowhere to put them. It is a state of affairs that brings laughter when it does not bring tears.

The Non-Co-operatives grow in number. The poor people who are ignorant and unlettered and know only what is told to them, are at the mercy of the Political Agitator. They hear first this, then that, and know not what to make of any of it. In every mob are large numbers of people who have no idea at all what it is all about, and in any lathi charge, these are they who get their heads broken, which stirs up further strife, for it is not difficult to bring it home, even to the unlettered, that this is not fair.

On the day of one of our great boycotts about the Simon Commission, I visited a Mohammedan friend who kept a silk shop in which he does much business with Tourists and people off ships who come with money to spend. I find his doors closed, and upon the front of his shop this large poster hanging, to say

"SIMON GO BACK."

"So," I said to him, "you also now take a hand in political matters, even to the spoiling of your trade."

"Sir," he said, "what can I do? Simon I never heard of, and there is a Tourist ship due in at noon, which would be very propitious for trading. Yet, if I open my shutters, it has been told me I shall get my shop looted and smashed up."

[115]

So marches the great Indian nation to what they call freedom.

Do you see that my old acquaintance Mr. Nigel Hill has been made a Knight in the Birthday Honours, and is now also Governor of the Northern Provinces? No doubt I shall see him again some day, since he will come often to Delhi, where my duties will take me also from time to time.

Is it not strange to look back, Lady Sahib, and to consider that once upon a time, for the reasonable sum of Rs55/- cash down, I might have changed the whole destiny of the Northern Provinces! Life is certainly a strange game, for he, who never liked me, did me a good turn, and I, who had it in my power, at least abstained from doing him a bad one! And now, many years later, we see the results of it all working out.

Like the threads that go to make the pattern in a carpet, we are all mixed up with one another, black men, white men, and yellow men. One pulls a string, and cannot say what the reaction will be. And never can we get any idea, ourself, of what the pattern we are making is in the end to be. That is for those who come after us, and shall see the results of our labours spread behind them over the years.

I like to think that through my pattern there runs a small golden thread, that makes it really quite smart, and that is your kindness to me, and your understanding, and our friendship and all that it has meant.

XXV

Most unexpectedly here I am, in the green and pleasant land of Burma again, where I first came as a boy so full of those magnificent dreams and his own importance as a social pioneer. . . . Well, it did not come to much after all . . . Burma has got on quite well without me. Here are the same large and unlikely blossoms upon the trees. Blossoms that must always suggest to me a little the unearthly flora that bloomed on the wallpaper of my rooms in Cambridge. About the Pagoda slopes the same erections of bamboo and coloured paper. At present it is a wonderful Tiger, really very lifelike, so I suppose another Priest has died and will presently be burnt up from Tiger's inside.

The town itself I find much changed. Much building and improving of roads. Splendid buildings along the water front, now quite dwarfing the old ones which once looked so imposing. White stone buildings with green domes, with green tiles and fancy works upon them. But the old open drains I see still exist. I see and am aware they still exist! And once off the main streets, the old squalor and dirt reigns supreme, with many dogs suffering from the misery of mange.

There are now so many motor cars at four in the afternoon, and so many European policemen standing here and there at cross roads, under little umbrellas, to conduct them that one could almost picture oneself somewhere in the West.

Much of the green and pleasant jungle that was here when I last came has gone, transmogrified most horribly into acres full of small red brick villas. Yes, villas, the worst possible members of the villa family. Never shall I take kindly to red brick. It is not a building material very suitable for the tropics. But they tell me the Government has started some brickworks here, and of course, to make the brickworks pay, houses must be built. . . . And on the story goes.

They tell me all this elaboration of buildings is to do with the University. Many there are that say because of this colossal undertaking and all its ramifications, the Province dithers unpleasantly close to bankruptcy. Of that as yet I cannot express an opinion. But this at least I know. The art of the Burman lies in his hands, and not in his head. If the University is turning out more lawyers, unpractical engineers, or seekers after Government jobs with pensions—then it is a sad affair for Burma.

I have come over here to sit on a Committee enquiring into the causes of the Rebellion which has stirred this once peaceful place into such a ferment all the last Cold Weather. The trouble is an old and pitiful one, of a people whose grievances have become too large to be borne. Of a people who have found it pays better to join in a band with sticks and knives and go out at night and marauder—than it does to sit at home and work and pay taxes too large for the family exchequer, and listen to the voice of the agitator and the Bolshevik Agent when he comes along.

The East is so terribly poor. She is ready now to listen to any quack who comes along with a medicine promising her quick relief from at least some of her pains, without enquiring too closely into what the medicine is made of.

The rice cultivator has gone from bad to worse, and now raises his crop almost at a loss. Only the Bania[1] and the Chetty flourish in this land. At last there is a movement on foot to reduce a little, the taxes. But it has come a lot too late.

[1] Money-lender

Nor can it be reduced very much, because, as one of my colleagues remarks, "We have got to have the Revenue to keep things going at all."

The expensive salaries have to be paid. The roads, begun, have to be finished. And there it is. So is slowly strangled the goose that once laid golden eggs. He no longer remains at home attending to business. He has become a ravening beast wishing only to destroy, to plunder, and to burn. He sees only that he must pay, pay, pay, all for things that bring him personally no advantage, for amenities that will never reach his township in his time. The small man in the jungle sees this, and becomes fed up. Many there are who make a point of going about, and rubbing it well in.

So there has been a rebellion. Such a pitiful rebellion it was, mostly of very young boys who made for themselves secretly a uniform, and tin helmets fashioned from oil tins belonging to the Burma Oil Company, and spears with their ends composed of this same useful material. And sometimes they come on foot in bands, and sometimes they come against the Police and their rifles riding the village ponies . . . and as long as the sun shines upon their tin helmets and makes a little glitter, they are glad and brave, and really believe they can overthrow the Government. Men who should know much better are blinded equally by this glitter, and encourage the youths to go on.

For Burma is a land of Pantomime, pretences and spells no more real than those the Christmas Fairy can wave out of her wand in the theatre in London.

It seems almost heartless to send against them sensible folk armed with real guns. Yet believe me it has been very necessary.

Besides their tin helmets to protect them, these rebels wear on their arm spells, which have been sold them in the Hpoongyi Chaungs, and are guaranteed to hold the wearer proof against cut from knife, or from rifle fire.

For after binding the spells upon these youths' arms, it is the custom for the vendors of this uneasy magic to fire at them three or four times from a blank-cartridge pistol, after which the initiate, seeing he is unhurt, is imbued with a great courage. I have talked with an English Policeman, who has been out in the jungle rounding up these rebel bands. He told me:

"How can I have the heart to tell my men to fire. These boys come towards us, taunting us, waving handkerchiefs. Telling us to shoot, because, they say, we are gun-proof, and you cannot hit us. And then they fall."

He told me, this same Policeman, that he visited in the Hospital one of these youths who had fallen, and talked at some length to him on this subject of supposed charms.

"You can now see," he pointed out, "what this bought magic is worth."

Like Mala and her Mother, the young man would hear nothing against the old system. Not even his own disaster helped him to see through it.

"In my case, the medicine was not good. There was something amiss. Perhaps I bound on my charms on a date that was inauspicious. The others," he said, "they are gun and knife proof. You shall see."

Yesterday I went up to Toungoo. . . . All along the distant sides of the hills came smoke from the burning villages. In the railway stations, armed Police patrolled here and there, looking a little uneasy. There are many distressing murders reported every day, and to look for several bands of dacoits in the jungles of lower Burma, it is like looking for the proverbial needle in the stack of hay. We know where they have been, but not where they have gone.

Sometimes news comes of their arrival at a village, but before the authorities can get permission to take drastic steps to surround and deal with that village, they are gone. The machinery of the law and of the Western administration is too cumbersome for this emergency. Where you can get about quickly on rubber tyres over reasonable roads, yes, it is a very good idea.

Here in my heart I know we require somebody like Mr. Chelston or the soldier about whom he told me, prepared to act on their own initiative and risk the consequences. To me, as an onlooker, it seems that everyone who should be about and doing something is awaiting for an order over the telephone and does not yet realize that the wire has already been cut.

XXVI

I HEAR to-day the story of a young Englishman, assistant in some business here, who obtained ten days' leave, and duly departed on a shooting trip, alone with one Burmese servant, one Native Shikarri, into the Pegu Yomah's.

When he has been gone only four days, the Pegu Yomah's and neighbouring villages begin to seethe with this rebellion, headquarters being at Thayetmyo, and many fires, murders and sackings of villages taking place everywhere.

Imagine the feelings of this Firm, considering that in the midst of all this trouble is one promising young Assistant, taking some holiday. To all lengths they have gone to get in touch with him. Runners are sent out, but cannot find him. The Thayetmyo Police are on the lookout. This young man's description is sent all over the District.

But the days pass, and nothing materializes, and he is now spoken of kindly, as they speak of the dead, and a telegram is prepared to send to this young man's sorrowing parents at home.

When this had been agreed upon, who should come walking into the office in the early morning, than this young man himself, very brown, very pleased with everything. Ready to get back to work.

"But where," they ask him, "have you been all the time?"

"Shooting in the Pegu Yomah's. Very excellent sport," replies he.

"Then you have not suffered in any way at all from this Rebellion?"

"What Rebellion?" says he, and is much aghast at what he now learns. For keeping only to his launch on the waterways, he has been out of touch with all bringers of news. In the mountains, he said, there was nothing that appeared amiss. Sometimes it is true he met large armed bodies of men moving here and there, but knowing nothing of trouble, he said he hoped they had had good sport, thinking them hunters like himself. In every case, he says, they laughed in most friendly fashion, and agreed that they had had excellent sport.

So he came through the centre of the trouble, and knew nothing about it at all. Yet in this same District was one Englishman killed only last week, and as yet we have not been able to discover what has been done with his head. The rest of him is already to hand, and has been accorded decent burial.

XXVII

Now we have hundreds of rebels here waiting for trial on various charges of murder, arson, and such things. They are momentarily housed in a disused cinema at Government expense. Many of them are to receive pardons for reasons of policy, not justice. If we exterminate so many of the young men, who is to plan next season's rice crop? Who is to carry on?

So up to date nothing has been done, and we have only had one trial. This is the trial of an honest, according to his lights, Burmese Policeman. Sad is his tale. All fired with zeal, he went about his lawful business of rebel hunting, and became mixed up in a fight in which many were taken prisoner, I understand. When it was over, back goes friend Burman licking his wounds to headquarters, and finds on the way, a rebel fallen by the wayside, pretty severely wounded, and still armed.

So he has questioned him a little about this and that and the other. Probably not very politely, but that I cannot say. And after that he has shot him—a course which in the case of an animal would have been highly commendable.

Now he is to be tried, this man, for murder. It is a most complicated case, and I am glad it is not for me to sit on it. For surely it was a better death than to lie and see, one by one, the vultures arrive, and sit around, waiting!

It is not a nice plot for a Gilbert and Sullivan play? Is it not Topsy-Turvey morality? As a young man, I remember when I first saw the *Mikado* I was often at a loss to understand why many people laughed!

Also to my notice has come another slight anomaly.

This was the case of another young man, who ran to earth a rebel band and despatched them all five, being a very courageous young man and one who should go far in his profession. Now it has been especially asked of all Officers that they identify without fail all their prisoners, since otherwise it will not be known when the ringleaders have been caught.

This young man was four days' march from any sort of Police Station or headquarters, and the weather was at its hottest. He had with him but a handful of the faithful, and there was no means of identifying the deceased, nor yet of getting their bodies back to where they could be identified, in a very salubrious condition.

So talking the matter over with the men in his small company, and no doubt advised by them to adopt this ancient and honourable custom of the country, this young man proceeded to remove the heads of his dead enemies, since so much of them he could hope to carry back with him. He returned to Headquarters in the good old-fashioned style of the conqueror, half a dozen scalps dangling at his saddle.

So the Authorities are able to be sure that a ringleader was amongst them, and need be sought no more. Having done this, they then round on the young man with one accord, and loud voices of horror are upraised against him, whilst in Assembly, mouths spout veritable Niagaras of hot air, regarding this atrocity.

And whilst it goes on and on, and for a time looks as if law and order must lose a very valuable and useful member on this point of etiquette, behold, in the jungle, and around the villages, the small men kneel and prostrate the forehead into the dust with respect at this man's name, and pray for his coming that they may garland him with flowers. In my own heart I believe his action has probably done more to bring in sight the end of the troubles here, than the threatening companies of soldiers.

For here you cannot get away from it, Lady Sahib. Many things there are that are simply too hard for the small man in the village, or the evil man behind the hpoongyi chaung, with a knife, to understand at all. The significance of red tape, it is nothing to him. But a head hanging from the saddle, that is a thing anyone can understand, being quite simple and to the point.

Amongst all this talk, all these conferences and enquiries, the unlettered man sees nothing of justice, or of mercy. Only weakness and fear. Amongst the elders in the meeting places the words go forth:

"The Swan, they say, has flown away. The Tiger has made the Crow his Minister."

Which is to say, you see, talk, and nothing else. Caw, Caw. But a few heads hanging from the saddle and they say, "Behold, the Swan has returned."

In my heart I can find it to agree with them, shockingly easily. But then, I have already told you, it takes three generations to civilize the

heathen. And I am only the second generation. Otherwise of course I also would recoil
from the severed heads, and bow to the scarlet
tape.

XXVIII

Do you remember how I wrote to you of this wedding in my family last year, Lady Sahib? To-day we hear this little Bride has died, endeavouring, and signally failing, to give birth to a son.

Little girls of ten are not intended to give birth to sons. How hard I have tried to do something for this poor child. To my Cousin I wrote many letters when I hear of the coming event, beseeching him to take this child to the Hospital so that at least she may have a fighting chance for her life.

But, no. In the small hut behind the house, alone with the Dhai, she has faced her hour, alone, because she is, under these circumstances, unclean.

Are we not a nice people, Lady Sahib? And some of our quaint customs, are they not very pretty? I am turned a little sick at my own helplessness amongst so much misery. Almost it were better not to see—to drift with the tide, to be lulled, with the rest of my people, into a coma, by the chattering of the old woman.

[133]

I can do nothing.

But my eldest girl, she is to study Medicine presently. She will be able to go to the other side of the Zenana curtains. And perhaps there also, in three generations, a little common sense may begin to sprout.

Only it is such a long time to wait.

XXIX

THIS disease of which I have told you, for building on such a lavish scale, has certainly affected the Gymkhana Club very badly indeed. In old days it seems always large and imposing enough. Now it is quite palatial. It is twice its previous size. The lavatories for the gentlemen there, are much more splendid than the High Courts, in their wealth of marble, their magnificence of window.

Surely something is out of perspective somewhere, when the lavatories become more magnificent than the High Courts!

Lately, in the Ball room that is all white and gold, with decorations that are very like those on the wedding cakes one sees in shop windows in Bond Street, I came across the man who was Commissioner at Myosein before Mr. Chelston. He has since then been made a knight, and is now called Sir Ralfe Cambourne, and his wife, this charming little Burmese Lady, she is now Lady Cambourne.

All their many children are still with them,

plain as the offspring of Anglo-Burman marriages seem always to be. It is a hard life for them, these poor children. The European community has no place for them, the Burmans also regard them as quite beyond the Pale. No one will marry their daughters, unless perhaps another half-caste, endeavouring to anchor his personal misery somewhere, and of that, her father would never hear.

It would be a good thing if legislation would forbid offspring to these mixed marriages—and if all persons contracting could be thereupon sterilized. Then let them if they wish to, spend their lives together. No one is jeopardised, no one will have to suffer. From marriages of mixed races, no super-man is going to emerge. I have a relation who is a Doctor in America. He tells me many things of this melting pot. From it, the super-criminal certainly emerges, but nothing else.

I dined with the Cambournes. Inside their house is a forlorn and dusty splendour that is full of echoes, and spittoons, and reclining Buddhas, and European arm-chairs, and book-cases of deep and learned books. Amongst this spiritual and temporal muddle, we sat and talked of old times, and it seems to me that Sir

Ralfe has lost much of his dislike for the damned Wog, and is almost prepared to own he may have, here and there, good points.

But alas, with the old prejudices, something else is also gone, and always I have the feeling that somebody has blown Sir Ralfe Cambourne out. That now he has hardly more than an echo of a man, sitting amongst his half-caste children, and the odds and ends of culture, Eastern and Western. This is not a good thing to happen to a person.

Also I am aware from what I hear that he is distressingly badgered. For the many relations of his Burmese wife, naturally they expect preferential treatment at his hands, in a country where not to assist your own is a greater crime than skilful robbery or hearty lying.

I must say I find the climate here both damp and enervating. Perhaps because I am no longer as young as I was. So many things have changed since I was last here, that it is almost like exploring a new City.

Yet one thing I have not found in any way changed. I walked beside the Lakes and came to the place where once I rowed all night looking for my small boy, Dravid. Where at length they brought him back to me, drowned, and I knew that never again would he climb on to my knee, and pulling off my glasses make me laugh by saying that in them I look like a large frog . . . The old anguish and bitterness of that time filled my heart once more.

The loss of a child, is it not the one thing that leaves a wound memory can never gloss over, and time even cannot heal?

Of Arvind I am getting good news now, thank you. He is working well, and is, perhaps, not so light-headed and easily blown by opinions this way and that. He is, they say, a boy of much promise, once he can learn to settle down. His political activities still cause me some uneasiness, and I do not altogether care for the company he keeps. Indeed, I wish I had sent him to England away from it all, but you who have just one son, will realize with what reluctance one parts from the First Born.

From the Districts, nothing cheering. More troops, they say, for India. That will mean more taxes, and that will mean more broken heads. . . . And Gandhi now hops in and out of prison, like the small man on the weathercock I once had at Cambridge, used to hop in and out of his front door. And nothing anybody says seems really to mean anything.

Meanwhile I am hard kept at it amongst my Files, Appeals, and Special Hearings, and can only hope that in our drunken staggerings we are somehow moving a little nearer the light.

xxx

To-day I hear with horror of this senseless assassination in the North. An Englishwoman and her two children most brutally attacked. It makes one sick to observe the enormities committed in the name of freedom. People who do such things should instantly be disposed of, as my dear friend would have said. Swiftly and effectively.

But instead, the malefactor is housed and fed and given time to air his poisonous ideas and to become a martyr, whilst at our leisure through many weeks we make pompous enquiry into whether he did that which we are certain he did.

I must not write to you any more about the difficulties I find, and about politics, or I shall weary you. I fear the subject gets on my nerves, for here we are in the thick of it, and no one can talk of anything else, which engenders a tense atmosphere which readily fills with brickbats. Mohammedans and Hindus keep us occupied with constant bickerings. It is noteworthy that

[140]

in this country the worst trouble occurs always in the Hot Weather, showing that without a doubt besides Financial considerations, the liver and inside economy of man plays a large part in his final destinies.

Now I must tell you only good news and pleasant things.

My son Arvind has passed his examination with much credit, and Honours, and is shortly to be gazetted on probation to some District, where he will begin his work. I hope he will remain in India, and for the present not go to Burma where nowadays there is so much upset and wild talk still. For Arvind, my son, is hot headed, with the unbridled enthusiasm of youth. He needs much restraining from pushing his rash conclusions too far.

My second son, John, goes to Cambridge next year. I am hoping to bring him over myself, and to see something of England again. No doubt there also I shall find many changes. Mala will not accompany me, for she is full of fear of the Black Waters, and also entertains many strange fancies about England. For someone has told her that there are no dogs in England. Only horses of all sizes, from small lap horses for the home, who eat with the family, to large horses, elephant size, for working the fields. Also, they have informed her, there is often frog rain, and worm rain, and bat rain, in England, these pests showering plentifully from the heavens. And how, says Mala, would I go, my hair full of bats, or worms, or frogs?

If I tell her that in the many years I resided there, I saw none of these wonders and marvels, Mala replies: "Ai, ai, but then we know this of my husband. Always my husband takes that country's part against his own."

Who should I meet in the Club the other day, but my old acquaintance Sir Nigel Hill, come to great honour and many Chuprassis with scarlet coats. Alas, he is as little my friend as ever, and entering the Club in his sight I am aware of becoming suddenly smaller, and smaller, until all the pleasant conceit I have had of at last being Somebody of a little importance, has departed through the toes of my boots.

Sir Nigel came down for a Conference. We sat on it together. How many are the Conferences? . . . Indeed I am often minded to say with the little man in the village, the small man beside the tank, that the Swan has flown away, and the Tiger taken a new Minister! Consider the League of Nations, that super-conference that I cannot very well understand, for it is a stupendous cost to the Taxpayer, and I cannot see yet what return he gets for his money. Some-one said to me recently about this, that it had done a great work with the White Slave Traffic.

This seems to me a little like turning out a regiment of soldiers to deal with the small boy cannon of little boys. Here in India we have Conferences on the Boycott, on non-Co-operation, on this, on that. And ever more we come out by that same door where in we went. And always one reads anew "A Committee has been appointed. . . ."

Mostly in my readings of History I have noticed that where there was a wrong, an army of the bravest took sword and banded themselves together to right it.

To-day, they take a fountain-pen, and make a note!

After that, they talk.

I spoke several times with Sir Nigel Hill. He is not changed. Time has done little for him, except give him a Knighthood and a lot of scarlet coated Chuprassis. He is a cold and distant man. Maybe to his own kind he can unbend a little and sometimes become human, but I have never seen it. Even in the Clubs he is always apart, his eyes half closed, looking on. Shut away from us all, with no idea of what goes on inside the heart of man, and no desire to know.

Government training out here is rather apt to do this to all of us. To dry up our humanity, and block our outlook with files, so that unmoved we are able to look on those who starve for food, or for understanding, and feel that if such a thing does not come under Reference 23c. it must be quite inevitable and we can do nothing about it.

Sir Nigel said to me. "A nice mess your country is in." He said it grimly, as if I had made it. "I remember telling you as a young man how little patience I had with it, and its ways. Now I have still less. . . ."

I told him I had little patience with the one-eyed political activities around us to-day, also, but from Sir Nigel's face I know in his heart he thinks I also am only a schemer for my own ends. So we talk a little, very much at loggerheads. I told him I thought this cat and mouse game with Gandhi did no good in the Districts, at which he laughed unpleasantly.

"You, no doubt, would like to see him Vice-roy."

I told him Gandhi had no aspirations to become Viceroy. But that Sir Nigel does not believe, and when he does not believe something, then the conversation had better be dropped for no one will ever convince him. I told him that to my mind there was a sad lack of consecutive policy. That I thought people will always follow any leader if he appears to be going steadfastly in one direction. But when leaders doubled and redoubled, and came back on their tracks, and went in the opposite direction for a while, only to turn again—then I told Sir Nigel, indeed the people will lose heart. They become weary and bewildered. They marauder on their own.

I talked to him of the topsy-turvey morality of the Burmese Rebellion, where we sat in solemn conclave to judge a Policeman who had tried so hard to help us—a course of conduct which to the small and unlettered man can only be translated as endeavouring to curry favour with the evildoer—of being frightened of the malefactor.

Sir Nigel showed me very clearly he did not consider it worth his while to discuss things with me. He yawned a little wearily, without taking too much trouble to disguise it.

"You and your kind are all Nationalists at heart," he said. "If I had my way, you would none of you be in Government employ. We must rule. Not tinker and play around with experiments. What," he said, "would India be like to-morrow if we went?"

"Alas, sir," I said, "and what will she be like if, under present conditions, you stay?"

Whereupon Sir Nigel proceeded to cast grave doubts as to whether I and my kind, Government servants of some position, were ever loyal to the system they pretended to uphold, and he said that a great deal of our present troubles came from just that.

I said to him "Be that as it may, then for the sake of argument, let us look at another point of view. You do not care for the Indian in the Administration. You say they are not loyal because everywhere they are not strongly in favour of all the laws of the West. What then, about the Irishmen? Many Irishmen out here are openly anti-British, and go to great pains to say so. The Irish are doing all they can to sever connection with the British Raj. Yet here he is, employed in his hundreds in all the Services. In my time I have known many Irishmen, hating England and making no bones about it—with the other hand drawing from her their pay and allowances. Surely," I said, "this is a more unreasonable and renegade measure than the employment of Indians in what is, after all, their own country, and amongst whom you must find a certain amount honestly desiring her welfare."

But on that Sir Nigel said I must remember Irishmen were white men, and consequently in every way more reliable, and better balanced mentally, and straighter than black men. He also informed me I talked wildly and without proof.

So the subject dropped between us, because Sir Nigel did not wish to discuss it any further.

Before we parted I told him of my pleasure as a young man, when I found he had given me such good reports on my work, and I told him I was aware how much his reports on me had helped me on.

He replied in his cold voice he had no complaints as to my work at any time. That I had always appeared to be an efficient officer.

"Yet," I said, "our time together in Myosein was not a success."

He replied candidly, "No. I hate your damned country, Nehra, and everything in it. It is no use mincing matters and pretending I don't."

"I wonder why, in the first instance, you wished to come to it?" said I.

Then Sir Nigel replied as before. "A man must live. In another few years, thank God, I shall be done with it. I shall be very glad to be done with it, and its eternal wranglings and upheavals, and bad smells."

So you see, Sir Nigel indeed pursues a very conservative policy, and even time and experience, that sometimes soften men's hearts, does little for him.

It was for me an interesting evening, although I am well enough aware that in speaking with me Sir Nigel disregards some of the smaller courtesies he would have observed with his own kind—or even if an Irishman, however disloyal. Here is a man I admire greatly for his ability, but cannot like. If he and I could like one another, and work as friends, therein would lie, I fancy, the salvation of my poor country, since all our energy would flow in one direction.

It was upon the end of my tongue to tell Sir Nigel how once it had been in my power to assist him summarily out of my damned country once and for all, for a very reasonable sum of say fifty-five rupees.

I refrained. I am not at all sure Sir Nigel would see any joke. And if Sir Nigel took it seriously, it might be troublesome for me, who am now a Judge of the High Courts!

XXXI

FOR another Christmas letter I must thank you, also for some books, which I shall read and enjoy. What a kind friend you are. I am so glad you are interested in the old volume of Indian Tales I have found for you, and a little surprised that it should have all the value you say. I picked it up here in the Bazaar.

The Hot Weather will shortly be upon us again. Already in the compound about my house, the loud Coppersmith bird toils, setting an example of diligence I cannot follow. There has just arrived here, to the pleasure of the children, a large hoopoe. Do you remember from your sojourns in the East, this handsome chap? Do you know our Eastern story concerning him, that he was once King Solomon's messenger? One day King Solomon was oppressed by the heat of the sun, and the Hoopoe came and made for him of their wings an umbrella and a sheltering.

So pleased was Solomon he said to these birds, "Ask anything you wish, and I will give it."

Foolish indeed were they, and asked to be

allowed to wear a golden crown just like his. So each hoopoe went out with a golden crown, and were immediately set upon and slain in great numbers by the avaricious, who hitherto had not considered them worthy of attention.

What wisdom lies in some of these ancient tales, Lady Sahib!

XXXII

LIFE goes on here, with many boycotts, many assassinations, more talk than ever, and still greater numbers of people waiting at the end of the telephone for a message that cannot come through because the line was cut some time ago. And we are to have another Conference, and this time the table will be round. Gandhi, who for a short time has been quite a hero, visiting in High Places, is once more cast into outer darkness.

For the English, Gandhi is only another joke. At a dinner party recently at Government House, one of the A.D.C.s said to me, "This is a cunning plan, to send Gandhi to England. Because, if he goes there wearing only his loin cloth in November, he will certainly die of pneumonia and then there will be peace, since the jolly old climate of jolly old England, is not favourable to jolly old loin-cloth wearing."

He is such a nice young man, that I cannot say anything more about it, but only laugh with him.

[152]

I was so interested to hear that in spite of all the gloom and forebodings of some of the family, Young David is to enter the Civil Service after all, and to come out here. I see it with you, and believe that never was a time when the East had greater promise for a young man. A young man prepared to come out to us, with none of the old inhibitions, but to work with the people here in kindliness and friendship: who will not expect us to remove ourselves from the same sidewalk, or place the forehead upon his feet, and come into his presence only shoes in hand. A young man, who cannot remember how ever upon the topmost tower of Lucknow the banner of England blew—to whom the Black Hole of Calcutta is only a story someone has told him, without bitterness, as one can tell these stories long, long afterwards.

For such a one, never have the gates been wider open. I cannot but believe that your David, bringing to it something of his mother's tolerance and kindness of heart, and broad outlook on the hats and foibles and customs of other men, will succeed where so many fail for just the lack of these qualities. Do not keep back from us your young men. Perhaps when the time for them has come to work with us, they will, after all, not find us so bad. There are, I gather, unpleasant masters to be had in England also!

I was indeed happy when I hear David is to be at Cambridge at the same time as my son, for —who knows, Lady Sahib?—might they not between them in their own small corner of the world, lay a foundation stone for better understanding between the East and the West, which must come, but meantime tarries by the wayside?

Arvind has now his first job. It is far from what I could have wished. Fate, that so loves, I think, to make a sport of us poor mortals, has sent him up to Sir Nigel Hill's Province, where he will come into touch with much I also found so difficult and disheartening in my early years.

Sir Nigel Hill is not the man to inspire the young with a desire to follow until death. Rather is he apt to depress them to that dead level of despair when nothing seems very much good, and so what we do, is of little importance.

Perhaps, presently, I shall be able to pull some strings and have him removed to a more hopeful place for him, at least in the beginning, until he is a little settled down. Is it not strange how all through my life and my career, this man must come into touch with me some way, either personally, or through my sons? You see, Lady

Sahib, he is a thread in my pattern that I weave, and I, perhaps, am also a thread in his.

If there could only be found somewhere a man like my dear Mr. Chelston, to start my son on his way. Alas, at Sir Nigel's age Mr. Chelston was still a Commissioner of a forgotten and unimportant district in Burma. I often wonder just what it is brings a man to prominence and success, since it is so rarely that true merit and talent that would have been so much use to him. Sometimes, Lady Sahib, it is in my mind to think that amongst white races also, the favouring of one who is relation, or friend is not entirely unknown.

I wonder what you think personally about this?

XXXIII

Do you remember some time ago I wrote to you of our difficulties out here with Irishmen who held important posts under Government, and yet in their hearts have no love for England, and no loyalty, and work against her secretly and in their own fashion, with considerable hatred?

To-day there came up before me in my own Court, such a case. It came before me on Appeal, and was that of a young Englishman, an officer in one of the Regiments, who, driving his motor car home one day, had knocked down an Indian and unfortunately at a later date, this Indian died.

The Irish Judge who tried this case, did so with prejudice that was disgraceful and made at the time many disparaging remarks about the Army, nicely calculated to tickle the ears of that Party out here always waiting for such news. He imposed on this young man a sentence ferocious and out of all proportion to the offence, for the young man was admittedly not driving fast, and the Indian was elderly, drunk, and deaf.

So it was for me, who am an Indian, to set this
sentence aside and allow the appeal.

Whereupon you can picture the mischief this
Irishman who endeavours always to curry favour
with the National Party here, and to be their
friend above any considerations of real justice—
has made amongst my own people, pointing the
finger at me as traitor to my own cause. Believe
me, Lady Sahib, here is a type of official we could
very well do without.

You have no doubt read by now of our Salt
Makings. What a sorry farce, isn't it? And now
over this matter our Hospitals are full of freshly
broken heads, and loyal hearts burning with fire
and ill-feeling, and the prisons full to bursting
point, so that often real crime must be winked at
a little because we cannot deal with it.

I think we badly need an all-round simplifica-
tion, for a vicious circle arrives, in which the
money taken to pay these taxes is more than
absorbed in dealing with the rows that arise over
their collection.

Meanwhile, New Delhi must be seen to be
believed in the splendour of its marble pillars,
its palatial buildings, its gardens and its terraces.
And round the jungle go the stirrers up of
trouble, saying to the little man in the villages,

the small man squatting beside the tank, "Why should you pay for all this? Up, Brother, and smash someone's head. They take your money for these matters."

Too much expensive legislation, too many faddist notions, too many large and imposing buildings—those are at rock bottom the troubles in India, to which we give so many and such varied names.

I had hoped so much to get away to England this summer and bring my son John to Cambridge and see him started there. But alas this is not to be. So troublesome are things out here that for the moment all leave is stopped and how long this will go on for, I cannot say.

Perhaps you will be kind and tell your David that in the Autumn term there will be a young man with a black face, standing beside a doorway, feeling lost, and rather frightened and very much alone in a strange land.

XXXIV

THAT you should take all this trouble for my son, and now write to me so kindly about him, Lady Sahib, means more to me than I can ever tell you, and I do not know how I am ever to thank you for this.

I am well aware of the difference it has made to him that you are there in those first days when he is trying to settle down and adapt himself to so much that is new. To get first-hand news from you of him in these early days, assuages all those griefs and anxieties a parent must always have when children leave home for the first time.

You do not say whether it was entirely on his behalf you took this journey to Cambridge, but knowing your kindness of heart as I now do, I am well aware it may have been so, and I can only pray that the most powerful of the many Gods ingenious men invent for themselves, may reward you for all you have done for us.

John writes cheerfully and with enormous enthusiasm about it all, and I, who as a young man trod the same path, know how much easier it has been for him, arriving to find a friend in a new land of strangers. His great admiration for your David fills many sheets, and I read with such interest of this little boy whose growing and developing I have watched so long from afar, now arrived at manhood.

As one grows older, most of one's pleasure is bound up in one's children. The fires of ambition for us burn low, for we realize how many things can never be. It is now at our children's triumphs and successes we must hope to warm the hands. I no longer look for much to happen in my day. Already I become a little tired, a little disheartened at the ragged business men make of this life. Already I incline to turn to the ancient beliefs of my own people, that here we journey only for a little space, and shall continue, in other spheres, the work begun.

But for my sons, as the Americans say, there is no measure to my hopes. The Sky is the limit.

Of Arvind we have still quite good news, although I fear like me he finds Sir Nigel none too easy a task master. Still, in the meantime I shall do nothing. The young must find their feet, and must realize life is not always easy and to be achieved without any effort.

My wife died in the spring. Poor girl, she had

[160]

grown of late years so stout that she got about little. Life was dull for her, so it was a merciful release. I have my daughter to keep house for me. She studies to become a doctor, which pleases me, for little progress can be made out here until the women become more enlightened, and only by women can this be done, since no man other than the husband can enter the Zenana.

Though to-day more and more women are putting away the veil and becoming a little emancipated, it will take many years before we can meet them on terms of equality, as men and women meet in the West. Tradition dies hard, and always at the back of their minds remains the conviction that it is better to be the mother of a son, than to have a seat in the Assembly.

And then, there are the old women. The old women who wish to rule the home. Who will not let go.

XXXV

At the time of writing I suffer from considerable surprise, for I find I am also to come to England on this Round-Table Conference, since he who was to have gone from this District is fallen sick.

Now I am told I must go in his place, and I do not feel the choice is a wise one. I am no advocate or lover of conferences, whatever the shape may be of the table. I have in my time listened to such spates of talk, such Niagaras of Hot Air—and how little has come of it all.

The bright spot in the affair is that, coming to England I may at last see you again—and shall also have the opportunity of seeing something of my son.

From the masses of literature and Agendas sent for my consumption, little really emerges. We try to settle by talk that which can never be settled by talk in this world. I wish I approached the adventure with greater zeal, but once again I have the conviction that we are like so many small mice, turning with diligence at our ornamental water wheel, and the evening will not find us any farther advanced than the morning left us.

But this is the wrong spirit, of course, in which to approach such a beautiful Conference, at a Table that is to be completely round.

The English newspapers, I see, have much fun with Gandhi and his loin cloth, and his goat. To send him over at all, what a mistake. Whatever one feels about Gandhi, and the worthiness or otherwise of his cause, the fact remains this prophet is more suited to our climate than to yours, and it is sad to make a sport of one who is sincere, however, misguided.

As for the harm he does, it is no more than your Mr. George Lansbury, who speaks so knowledgeably about the Indian situation, never having been here, and knowing of it nothing at all. Your Mr. Maxton, whose utterances are reported in every small vernacular paper, so that the small man in the village must always look doubtfully on a justice that leaves unbroken his head.

India to-day wants statesmen to pull her together, men with fire in their heart so warm that its rays go out to other men, and embue them also with courage, and a sense of that vocation to a task, without which men do so little that is of any use.

Instead, there come to her worthy men with quack medicines, or amusing gadgets, or little men with their personal eye on a pension, playing meantime martial tunes on whistles.

Herein lies the tragedy of to-day. If there was anyone to follow, I think as of old, Indians would follow until death if needs be. We are at heart a romantic and easily moved people.

But no one comes. Only a comic face grimacing from a Punch and Judy Show, or here and there a Jackanapes in a toy helmet, on a circus horse!

XXXVI

OUR letters crossed each other, mine telling you I come to England, yours announcing your departure to China, the one unexpected as the other. So the Colonel Sahib takes soldiers out there, to settle yet another war.

I could wish you would be in some place more peaceful than China, but would be at a loss nowadays to discover that place, since about the corridors of the whole world there seems to-day to be nothing but the echoes of ancestral voices prophesying war!

So after all these years the nearest we shall come to another meeting will be to pass at sea and exchange telegrams. I have looked carefully into this matter and by no skilful combination of ships can I manage to arrive in Aden, Port Said or Marseilles at the same time as yourself, which I would much have liked to arrange.

It looks, therefore, as if my hopes of seeing you again were born only to fade. I shall, however, at last meet your son, and be able to thank him personally for all he has done for my boy. What a difference it has made, this having a friend at court, to a young man in a strange land. From John's weekly letters I am well aware of it. That he should have taken my son with him to London during the vacation, has made him so proud and given him so much pleasure. You could not guess at it without seeing his letters to me.

I shall be glad to get away from this atmosphere of warring communities, broken heads and intrigues for a little while. So much that reads in the papers like political trouble, means no more than that the Hindus are getting a dig at the Mohammedans. The Mohammedans getting a counter-dig at the Hindus. It is difficult for those living out here not to take advantage of the general unrest to repay old scores! Sometimes one's brain spins so that where is right and where is wrong does not readily emerge. And the wild cat schemes for this and that, the reckless spendings and buildings, advance unchecked, all sanctioned and approved by those who must surely, from their wisdom, see whither we tend?

I shall return East again in the early spring I think. It will be most interesting to have your impressions of a country about which I have read much, though apart from occasional merchants out here, I know few of her people. I gather her problems, like so many, work down to finance, and her difficulty is how to dispose of large armies accustomed by the results of loot and pillage to doing themselves handsomely—without continuing eternal wars?

I have always remembered Myosein jail, and how it contained representatives of all nations, only no Chinamen, and Mr. Chelston said, "This is not because they have not done anything wrong. It is only because they are too clever to get caught."

Poor America is now in the doldrums. From my cousin out there I hear everything has slumped, and even amongst his own patients and followers, nineteen who were only yesterday millionaires are now paupers. Very few people now come to my cousin, he informs me, to learn Eastern wisdom and practise the Lotus seat and breathings, and things are very bad. The problems of the rest of the world have arrived at America—unemployment, and slump and bank crashes everywhere.

It is, so my cousin says, very disastrous, because this is a young people, still with the minds of children. And as children in adversity suffer in comparison with grown-ups, having no ability for foreseeing a better to-morrow, and appreciating how transient is ever woe—so do the Americans suffer in comparison with the older races, childishly and pitifully. They have always been accustomed to being so pleased with themselves, and their buildings that are higher than any other buildings, and their cities which are larger than any other cities.

But now, their troubles, which are far larger than any other nation's troubles, they do not enjoy so much, and sit, says my cousin, in the meantime stunned. Too shocked even to get down to it, and deal with them.

This takes you all my best wishes for a safe and comfortable journey, and also my great disappointment at just missing you in this aggravating fashion.

XXXVII

To find oneself in Paris again after so many years, what a strange experience! Yet, in spite of world problems, I find Paris very little changed, even though since I last saw her she has been invaded, and suffered a great deal.

Perhaps it is adversity that keeps a country young, for certainly France has had plenty of adversity, and for all that I find her very girlish, very care-free and in a strange manner inclined to imagine that since the signing of the Treaty of Versailles, time has stood still. Since the signing of that dolorous treaty, France, I think, has stuffed the ears with cotton wool, and refusing to listen to the rebellious groans of the rest of the world, says to herself, "All is well."

Somehow, I cannot tell you why, I do not care greatly for the Frenchman. He is very friendly, he is very gay, and would never expect anyone to get off the side-walk for him or remove the shoe, I fancy, and for all this manifestation of good heartedness, remains the fact I do not like him.

Whilst I was in Burma I visited Saigon, and saw there a French administration. Side by side with the natives they live in a complete friendliness untinged with any vestige of respect. Their joys and their sins they share alike, partaking liberally of the native dishes and vices.

At the time I remember I fancied this was an excellent spirit. But then I was a very young man, smarting under the opposite of extreme of one Mr. Nigel Hill in Myosein. Now I am older and wiser, I can see only that for some reason this regime fills me with no enthusiasm. There is no forward movement, and from such communities come no great men to be leaders. And the Frenchman, I do not care for him. He annoys me when he stops me at the street end to show me postcards of a licentious nature, of the nude. That he cannot realize I, now almost a grandfather, must have lost most of my erstwhile interest and curiosity regarding the mechanical device of love—that he can never realize how after many years, love to most people becomes nothing much of importance, and has not the mystery even to make one wish to peep round the door, this annoys me like an affront to my intelligence.

To the Frenchman it appears, love is all. And it is all, all the time.

Often in the East I am come up against something of this mentality in the Censoring of the Films. How anxiously in Burma, in Bombay, in Calcutta, have they cut down the embraces, and curtailed the length of the kisses. Yet amongst the peoples for whom these moral steps were taken, it is as nothing, and less than nothing, since every child long before reaching maturity, knows all these things as a matter of course—since every temple is decorated and freely, with pictures no censor would ever pass.

Sometimes I have tried to tell these gentlemen concerned with the pictures, this. I cannot ever get it through to them. To them, immorality it is something to do with the body, and because it is so for them, they cannot see that for many people, it is nothing. So, protecting us carefully from knowledge of what we already knew from the cradle—they refrain from removing that which has really been harmful—the exploits of criminals, the wiles of the cat burglar—the hints of how to dispose of the corpse after a killing.

Disliking Frenchmen, I stayed at the Palatial. My window looked out on to a pleasant Courtyard full of waiters taking drinks to warm American ladies in small round hats. The fat, grey pigeon there have also the air of studying soon to become waiters themselves, as they waddle about taking notes on human behaviour. There were beautiful flowers there, a constant delight to me. Pink geraniums, and purple heliotrope, very sweet, growing as flowers will grow only in a temperate and kindly climate.

Although in France you may drink when you wish, I have seen very little of excesses. America, I gather, where you may not drink at all, is the most drunken country meantime, and in England, always it used to be the smart thing to become drunk in those hours of night and morning when it was against the law.

The Paris shops are so gay with their silks and pretty dresses and hats like bunches of flowers, and their *bijoux fixé*. I wish I could have brought Mala here one day, for how she would have liked these glittering things, who at heart was to the end just a child. Even though they tell me the time for spending much money is over, the Paris shops certainly have not lost heart, but sit here, dangling their baits.

There are so few English people here, and hardly any Americans, and those with whom I have spoken are full of gloom and wear the haunted expression peculiar to people who sit awaiting a cable that recalls them home to disaster.

Yet for all this depression the world seems to go on just the same, with marrying and giving in marriage. Many small children play as usual in the Bois de Boulogne.

Many pretty girls speak to me in the streets and whisper in my ear of novelties which make me wish to laugh, and at the same time, make me just a little sad.

That they could hope to teach me anything, who am by birth an Hindu, and also now a grandfather!

To-morrow I go to London. With strange mixtures of feeling I look forward to visiting again those places where it seems only yesterday I was a young man. So full of hopes and good intentions!

How little I dreamed then, of the circumstances under which I would be returning.

XXXVIII

OUT of the sea of talk in which I now flounder, I rise for a few moments to the surface, to breathe and to send you some news of this Great Round Table Conference upon which I now sit.

For many hours a day we sit and talk in sumptuous surroundings. We talk until the shadows lengthen and evening is here. And never do we decide anything. There is a warring of too many good ideas, and in the end, all it amounts to is that we have discovered yet fresh problems on which it is essential to Make a Note.

Presently I think we shall have collected so many problems that we shall be like the Professor in the French book "Penguin Island," and be submerged and buried beneath the masses of our dockets, papers, and agendas.

I listen and listen to wise talk, until my poor head reels. When it is my turn to ask a question, so weary am I, and so bemused, that nothing really seems to matter at all. My poor brain buzzes like a small bee in a large empty glass bottle.

Always, there emerges from it all one undeniable fact. Even if we all agree, even if the Safeguards go through and the White Paper's recommendations are passed and accepted, many Financial Experts have sat upon the matter for some time and are all agreed that it would not work. This edifice we propose raising, is in any case financially unstable. It simply would not work. So in the name of all that is common-sensical, of what use? Of what use?

Then also, the manner of our discussings!

To me come many of my countrymen, and say, "Yes. Of this I am entirely convinced. To give the Police Force and the Financial Departments entirely over into the hands of Indians themselves without supervision, that would be foolhardy and disastrous. But, my dear fellow, I cannot say so. I must vote in favour of it, because at home, it is expected of me. What will my position be on my return, if I do not advocate these things?"

So it boils down to the same thing once more. In the end, it is the small man in the village, the little man whose money we want, beside the tank, who rules even the Round Table Conference.

The wisest men have certainly been chosen, and the idea is good. Only the wise men come gagged with caution, and cannot use their wisdom because of their second thoughts, and financial considerations of what will be said in the towns at home.

"I would like to say what I really think. But, my dear fellow, if I did so, consider my position at home. A man must live."

That, I find is the general point of view here in London amongst my own people. To-day, with black or white men alike, there seems to be this one fundamental difficulty. Everyone has to live, and to that great need, more important issues are subordinated. Nobody remains who will take a Sporting Chance.

Often, looking about me in the Assembly here, I am struck with one conclusion, and that is that we are all too old, Lady Sahib. Amongst the distinguished Englishmen I see on every hand, are no young men. It is the young men we want, with friendliness in their heart, and the open mind. Who are able to conceive an India in which black men and white will work side by side, and white man be unappalled by the idea that some day a 'damned Wog' may be his official superior.

The old men can give us experience, but they cannot give us anything else, and all their experience deals with a state of affairs the Indian wishes to see in the past. They do not like us, the old men. They will never like us. The glory of the conqueror still hangs about them, and they remember good fellows who met horrible death at the Mutiny or were cruelly shot in the back in Frontier Wars. They remember only the happy day when the native was subdued and carried his head low.

It is the young man who does not remember, who never knew this old regime, from whom must come our help. I wish I saw him here upon this Conference. More vision we want, and not so much experience. You must not be angry at what I say to you. I speak my thoughts. Perhaps they are all quite wrong.

I stay, as you see, in an Hotel.

Mankind suffers under many delusions. One of them is that the telephone makes life easier! I am tormented with it here, even beside my bed. In vain I endeavoured to gag it by removing the receiver. A page then arrives to knock at my door and ask me why I have done this thing. And often when it rings, it is not even for me, but an enquiry for some purely nebulous Mr.

Brown, who inhabited these rooms before me.

I have here my own sitting room. Very comfortable. Only it is blocked with Files, Agendas, and papers of various colours. Had the day thirty-six hours, and I four pairs of eyes, I could hardly hope to digest all of them. It is becoming too much for the mind of man, this civilization, leaving him no time in which to walk about.

Incessant is the talk and the joking here over Gandhi and his goat. He is now become a music-hall joke, for the time superseding the great Mother-in-law pleasantry. "You make me feel as ill as when I see Gandhi's picture before breakfast," remarked the funny man in a recent show I have seen here. The audience was convulsed with mirth.

Many witty things also are said and hinted regarding his Ashram, but mostly they are of the sort I cannot mention to you. It is a pity there is no one to explain to some of the joke-makers that the Ashram is merely a school and *not* any sort of a Harem.

I am not the man to do it. As Mala accused me of prejudice towards this country, so would the jokers accuse me now of prejudice towards

mine. And also perhaps towards an Ashram—
or what they suppose an Ashram to be—which
is certainly something not very nice.

Such a sad mistake that Gandhi ever came
here. A worse mistake that no one causes him
now to hurry away, for what a nuisance he has
been to us, with his Silent Mondays, his scrupu-
lous observing of a law of the East in the
West, as unsuitable for it as his loin cloth is
unsuitable for the climate. Very clever, I think,
of Government to let him come. What better
proof of the inability of the Indian to govern
his own country, than this man, unable even to
adapt his garments to the local customs?

All he has done is to impede progress, to put
up yet another barrier between those we strive to
understand and they who strive, honestly I
believe, to understand us.

For us it is the same as for you. India also
needs Statesmen, and all she has is little men
insufficiently clad for the neighbourhood, small
men with some quack spells and magic, and some
goats.

XXXIX

HERE in London also I find a lot of talk about Financial troubles. Everybody has got them, and indeed I now seem to see in full play here that colossal machinery that grows yearly more and more expensive, against which my heart has always been turned in the East.

Could things be worse than here? I discover with a little simple calculation that in England to-day everyone must work one year in four, for nothing. Indeed I can only wonder there is no boom in gas ovens in which to place the head! One year in four for nothing—that would by no means be a popular idea with us out East. I meet in a private house, a private Indian gentleman not attached to any Government Department whatever. To me he says:

"You see what it is over here? With us, give them once the free hand, also it will come."

Too expensive. Also much too involved. All these beautiful gardens to be kept up around Government offices, all this brass to be polished, these unending offices with their regiments of employees, their hay-stacks of Forms and Regulations. It has been lost sight of, the great fact that to have an excellent idea it is not necessary to sit inside a marble palace! It is remarkable to consider how all the great deeds a nation does are done with the roughest implements. India was full of pioneers, when there were only mat huts for offices, and wooden buildings for Clubs.

But by and by, a man must build himself a splendid stone house, and inside it is so cool and pleasant his soul goes to sleep, and so the enemy creeps inside his gates.

I notice also here a great number of things done for no reason whatever except that they always have been done for hundreds of years, and so are become a species of Totem. Here and there for no reason one can discover, a custom has got left behind, and since it is so left behind, becomes holy.

A very kind lady has taken me only recently over one of your cathedrals here in London, and has explained to me some of the ceremonies that take place, and how on certain days there is a procession, and the Priest goes without, and knocks upon the door to be let in.

"But," I asked her, "is the door, then, not open to him?"

She became a little impatient and said, "Yes, yes. The door is open to him now, of course But once, you see, it was closed. Therefore he knocks."

XL

To-day I went into the City where I see many men wearing silk hats, and eating-houses rich with a profusion of pink lobster and beautiful red tomato. It must indeed be an inspiring thing to be an Englishman, able to eat freely and fully of the shrimp, the pig, and whatsoever may tickle his fancy, and no possibility of threats of eternal damnation instantly emerging from his Temple.

The silk hat, Lady Sahib, is surely the most ingenious and astonishing of all the headgears men have thought of. For most of them have at least some useful intention. The turban, it is to keep the effects of the sun from disturbing the brain. The fez, also, one can understand as creating a cool vacuum necessary to a hot climate.

But consider the silk hat in a snowstorm! Indeed, apart from the exercise achieved by running after it, as I saw no less than two persons doing in the high wind in Leadenhall Street, I can find for it no merit.

[183]

I have been down on some business to the Bank, which is beautiful as a Temple, all marble within, only in the place of the Altar, I saw only Cashier,—and instead of the preparation for a sacrifice, Income Tax Enquiries.

To deal largely with money, what an air it gives to any man. Here in this Bank each person holds the head high, like a King. Even he who, well decorated with many medals, stands at the door, regarding the sky so as to be able to tell the greater ones when they emerge, what the weather is going to do.

In the City I have seen also what I never saw before in any land, one large pure white moustache, the possession of an English gentle-man. It was large as a pair of rams' horns, and curled round and round at each end. It was, indeed, so very beautiful that I became mesmerised with admiration and must stand and stare.

And as I stand, to me approaches the Police-man, asking and not, I fancy, without suspicion, since I am so near a Bank, "Do you want any-thing?"

I wish very much to say to him, "Yes, I want very much to be able to grow such a moustache, of pure white with a little curl one at each side. And am sad, knowing I can never achieve it."

However, I ask him instead for a bus back to Westminster.

XLI

It has surprised me to find how much sedition goes on here in England herself. I cannot remember that it used to be so when I was here as a young man.

To-day I stopped for a while in Trafalgar Square. There was a crowd listening, both persons and pigeon. There was a small and somewhat unwashed-looking man speaking. He appeared to me to be but of low caste. (Has your country indeed no caste system, Lady Sahib? Think of this seriously!)

In some short space of time this man has said we must depose the Royal family, seize Buckingham Palace, deal with the Army and with the Navy. Indeed, he has presently said down with almost everything connected with law and order, and he has urged, quite passionately, the Workers to come On and Knock out the Police.

Close beside me, stood two Policemen. They appeared bored. They had the arms behind the back. They regarded only the pigeon, and once as I watch, one of them hides an almighty yawn behind a hand, and props himself for a short rest against a stone lion.

So I went and spoke to this Policeman, and asked how it was these people were allowed to stand up and say these wild things unrestrained, when in my country for the half of it many heads would have been split.

This Policeman was very large and very calm. He rocked himself upon his toes backwards and forwards and looked down upon me.

"It does them a power of good to get it off their chests," he said. "They just talks," he said. "That is all."

Indeed I must own that it seems for the moment to answer quite well, this great calmness. For nothing whatever happened. In Bombay at such a time there would have been shouts and lathi charges. There would have been broken heads. But all that happened here was before very long the small man seemed suddenly to tire, and he looked at his watch and dismounted from his high place. And all the other listeners there looked also at their watches, and someone said "Good-night, Bert" to the Policeman. It was all so friendly. Quite like a party. Presently the Policeman had the Square to himself and myself, and he regarded the pigeon very thoughtfully.

and me a trifle suspiciously, so that I also went away.

Being interested, I followed the small man for some way, and find that he is going to have his tea.

I have often thought it is this small and. comfortable meal that breaks so nicely the continuity of the afternoon's thought, that is the mainstay of the Empire. There sat our Fire Eater, with a woman of his own size, and hair cut. She was bullying him a little over something, I think, for he had an air that was a little hang-dog. As they had their tea, together they did sums on pieces of paper, so that there is borne in on me the suspicion that here again we are up against the same old problem of men having to live.

It may be somebody pays this small man to make his bad speeches, and that the rest of the crowd who gather, do so in the attitude of people going to the Pictures. To look, to listen, to be a little diverted until it is time for tea.

Not long after this I came across a procession of the Unemployed. They walked along the Embankment, looking tired. Presently a Policeman came. He was not unkind to them, for I gather there is no law against processing in England, just as there is no law against speaking

[188]

from elevated positions, and freeing amongst the multitudes whole Niagaras of hot air.

All the Policeman did was to head them off up a small side street where they did not wish to be. There seemed to be no difference in this Policeman's attitude to the poor and unfortunate, and those who wished to overthrow everything and urged the Workers to Come On and settle the Police. Perhaps because the heart of man is always kinder towards the positive, than the negative.

So I returned to my room and sat beside my fire, and wondered a little whether, left to herself, the East would make much worse a mess of her affairs than the West appears to be making. And to endure one's own mess, it is always better than to labour under the results of somebody else's good ideas.

The West has undoubtedly become spendthrift as a small boy whose Papa has always, and unwisely, given him unlimited pocket money and so encouraged him to suppose there is always plenty more where that came from, without anyone exerting themselves at all.

Here also, they are spending money the country has not got, it seems to me, just in the same way they are doing it out in the East.

In Geneva I hear of a Palace rising, so marvellous, so expensive and so involved, that now it is impossible for financial reasons to complete it.

This they call progress, but to me it looks like muddled thinking.

Daily our Conference goes on and on. I wish I did not feel it is all in vain. Talk will not drive the horse back into the plough, or turn adverse stars to send us prosperity.

Having thus talked ourselves into some form of stupor we are further stunned from time to time with magnificent banquets which put out of action very successfully any remaining faculties we may have.

I, for one, cannot greatly enjoy these affairs. For between me and my plate there comes the face of those men I saw on the Embankment, the faces of the young men I have seen, driven to crime in the Burmese Rebellion, the bewildered faces of the small men in villages, and squatting beside distant tanks. I feel that there is something very wrong, and alas, I am not clever enough to have a remedy, or even a suggestion. Only I know it gives me a discomfort within to drive along the Park in my friends' motor cars, and to see poor people sleeping there in the cold, using newspapers for their bedcoverings.

I have now been for six weeks in my Hotel, and so far not one person has spoken to me. The main population of this Hotel is old ladies. Very old, some of them, who march in the Park a little with a stick, and go a great deal to Church.

There is one old lady here whose hair-dressing is so clever I do not believe it can be quite an honest one. She holds herself very straight and sometimes, from the back, can manage to almost resemble her Gracious Majesty Queen Mary. Indeed, she has the air of being at least a queen, and not an old lady in a Private Hotel at all, only nobody had guessed her secret.

So imagine my surprise when one morning this old lady who for six weeks has not even managed to see me, stopped me as I entered the dining-room, and spoke to me without any warning.

And what she said was this:

"Mr. Nehra, do you know what day this is?"

After a little thought I can tell her, being acquainted with English festivals and fasts. So politely I replied it was Good Friday.

"And do you know for whom we pray in church to-day?" she continued, so severely that

I cannot for a time collect my thoughts. However, she did not wait for this.

"For Jews, Turks, Infidels, and Heretics, Mr. Nehra," said the old lady, and left me as suddenly as she had arrived.

Later in the day I noticed her departing, carrying a quite large book which is full of prayers, no doubt to do so again.

XLII

I HAVE been to some Theatres which amuse me and interest me a great deal, though I note in England to-day a tendency towards the morbid that I do not remember in those old gay Theatrical performances of my younger days. Always in the plays I see there are many complications, and most of them are disastrous.

It appears to me now that in France it is the naked woman that most amuses, and in England it is the tangled sexual relationship, whilst as far as I can make out from the one Russian play I have been to, in Russia nothing amuses greatly, only to commit suicide, and talk for at least three acts about it first of all.

The weather here has been quite marvellous for the time of year. In the morning it was so hot I ventured out without an overcoat, but presently it commenced to snow, so that I turned and hurried back, and reached my Hotel just in time to avoid a thunderstorm.

It is no wonder that the Western peoples are a calm and patient people, able to withstand much

[193]

that is trying, without fire in the heart. How could they be otherwise, reared in conditions like these?

In the Restaurants and Hotels I find with some surprise that in spite of all the unemployment, most of the waiters and certainly all the successful *Maître d'hôtel* are foreigners. It seems to me that this also is more so than when I was here before, and for a little while I am greatly surprised at it.

But after I have visited some of the remaining places where there are only English employed as waiters, then I can well understand. The Frenchman, the German, the Swiss and the Italian, he brings to the job of being a waiter, of arranging the table with flowers and concentrating upon the wine, the menu,—something of a dignity. Always he makes it appear impressive and distinguished, so that one understands it is the profession of his choice.

With the English, always they seem to have become waiters only by some sad accident, or to keep Hotels entirely through cruel reverse of fortune, or cessation of dividend. Always it is obvious they are filled with scorn for that which they must do to live. They infer, as they remove the soiled plate, that such matters are beneath them. All of them, I gather, were at least Colonels in the Great War, and it has soured the temper to have once been a Colonel and now to be one no more. They cannot get over this feeling that, instead of handing to you the soup they should be forming you into fours. And all the time they give the impression of a little despising you, which does not add to the fun of the party in any way, and in the end, you tip them too much with the air of one apologising, after which they despise you for so doing, and you depart, determined at least never to go there again.

With the foreigner, it is different. Indeed, for real dignity and impressiveness, I have been unable to find anyone to beat Mr. Ferrero at the Berkeley, as he walks about amongst his guests, in faultless clothes with his hands beneath his coat tails, seeing to this and to that. He is as a Prime Minister inspecting his Parliament. Always he has the air of being pleased to see you in his beautiful restaurant, and of hoping you will shortly come back again, so that almost it becomes a friendly matter, and many people there are in London who do not say "Shall we dine at the Berkeley?" Rather they say, I notice, "Let us go and see old Ferrero."

With those who are personally known to him, Mr. Ferrero will shake hands. It would be a proud day indeed for me, and one I would not forget, if Mr. Ferrero ever shook hands with me. I have seen in my day many Judges of the High Courts who for dignity and efficiency, and that air of being someone who is important, who really matters, who might do well to take a leaf from the book of Mr. Ferrero of the Berkeley.

XLIII

I NOTICE with much interest how the women of England can change shape at the dictates of fashion, adapting the person to the dressmakers' whim. To me this is quite amazing, for I am aware that no one could have adapted my poor Mala to any shape except her own. Here also I meet sometimes women of whom I hear the following day they have become Mothers during the night, and I have had no idea at all this event was even distantly in view. With us it is not so. Mala never left one in any doubt, poor girl.

How curious to my eyes are some of the women's fashions, also. These small hats that are placed in so odd a manner on the back of the head, exposing much of the face that were better unexposed, unless it is very young and new. The women of the West, to me they appear all so young. Also too thin to be well, and yet they appear so.

I go to Cambridge for this next week-end, my first opportunity to get away, and look forward so much to at least meeting your son. I have not yet been anywhere out of London, but I visited again the shop in the Opera Arcade, and there sat my old man. Indeed in almost thirty years he has grown no older, for evidently he had already reached, before I went away, such antiquity that further change was impossible. Sitting there in his small and rather dark shop, he remembered me at once, and the sort of silk handkerchief I like and produced some, I could swear it was from the same box.

He was a little despondent, my old man, and told me I had come to England at the wrong time, and that the country was indeed going rapidly to the dogs. All his life, he told me, he has tried to save money, but now he is not trying any more, but is spending what he has, because, he said to me, if you are thrifty and endeavour to make provision for those descended from you, at every turn you are penalized with large sums taken from you. But if you care to be thriftless and do not bother to look forward, then the Government will educate the children and pension the widow from the money they take away from those who work hard and endeavour to save.

It seems to me this is not a good plan, that

it is far from healthy to make people feel it does not pay them to be industrious and good. Here in the West, are they perhaps killing off their best class, to keep up and support that which is not so desirable?

XLIV

How much they talk in England to-day of the horrors of War. I attend innumerable lectures on it, also read many excerpts, and some there are who say that an attack by gas is to be very deadly, and others there are who say not at all, it will all blow away, and we can just shut the window until it has gone.

No one makes any great mention of the horrors of peace, yet I am told by those who ought to know that more people have been killed in traffic accidents since the Great War than the total casualties there amounted to.

That is a horrible affair. In War at least one goes forth prepared. One has a weapon and the expectation that something may happen, and one's affairs consequently left in good order. And if one dies, at least the death is an honourable one, and calls afterwards for kind thoughts, and calico poppies to be sold on one's behalf in memory of it.

Consider those who fall in Peace.

They are a small and unbelligerent people,

perhaps armed with nothing but the umbrella, the shopping list, when of a sudden they are mown down from behind or before. There is also no glory in their death, and many people write letters to the papers, saying they have no one but themselves to blame. Unsung they remain. No one retails their gallant effort of crossing the road with the lights against them. No memorial is thère, only a notice in the paper, for which the relations must pay.

Personally I would prefer to die in battle. Glorious to the end will be the soldier's death, and at least one has some run for one's money. One can bite back. But what revenge has the victim of the motor bus, as the tyre passes across his stomach?

I have just attended a splendid Socialist meeting where I hear that in the event of this form of Government once more returning, they would take charge of the Banks, and run them to the greater public welfare.

So much they say sounds sensible and good, and I have listened with great attention to Mr. Tom Watkins, M.P., obviously a man of considerable zeal. Much he says has so true a ring, that I come away a little convinced with this form of Government.

But unhappily then I come upon a newspaper in which I read that Mr. Tom Watkins, M.P., has sadly become bankrupt with liabilities of many thousands of pounds, due to extravagant living, and assets only one coat with astrakhan fur-collar and tenpence-half penny.

Is it not inevitable that I then ask myself some questions?

"Since," I say to myself, "Mr. Tom Watkins is so signally unsuccessful in the management of his own private affairs and finances, can he and his sort be particularly well fitted to handle those of a Nation? Since he has lost all his own money, in unwise and riotous living, is he the type who could be relied upon wisely to handle the Banks?"

It is to me an astonishing thing that a man chosen for high authority, even amongst en-lightened people, to-day is often not a man whose integrity and character is altogether beyond reproach, and I recall what once in India was to me something of a stumbling block at the time.

There arrived a new Judge from England and the first that we heard of him was he was fined Two Thousand Rupees for endeavouring to smuggle goods through the Customs and for making a false declaration upon his Customs forms on arrival.

At the time there was much talk, and in the Indian community of this place it was expected the Governor would take action and return this person as not very suitable to act in a highly honourable capacity.

Nothing happened, and there was much secret smiling and rubbing of the hands together, since it was then considered a good omen and that here would be a European Judge who could, in the way of speaking, be "got at" in the hour of need.

Lately I see this gentleman has also been Knighted, and perhaps one day I shall read that Mr. Tom Watkins has become Prime Minister, and is about to try and see what he can do with the savings of thrifty persons, now lodged in your Banks.

The world certainly seems to have got a little topsy-turvey in all parts. The more I consider things, the more I notice this tendency to place everywhere the power into the hands of those people who have no experience of same. The making of laws and the Government of the country is now chosen by the man in the street, who is on the dole, the girl in the shop, who has no knowledge or capacity for making any choices of importance.

It is in the hands of the great majority now. And the mentality of the great majority, in your country, and in my country, it is not a secret, Lady Sahib. They have nothing to lose, having themselves no stake in the business, nothing saved, and nothing planned. They can afford to encourage wild-cat schemes, since if it makes them no better off, at least it cannot make them worse off than already they have allowed themselves to become.

Here to-day it seems to me that the choice of law-makers and Rulers lies in the hands of the thriftless and inefficient, rather than the hands of those who know what they are about—the sort of people whose hand is readily outstretched towards the brickbat. And amongst the law-makers are many who consider only the money to be had from this job, and do not even keep the laws they make.

Can those unable to manage their own affairs do any better for a Country, is the question I ask myself.

Is this, in fact, what the Western administration would do in time for the East also? Transfer the power to the hands of the illiterate and

uneducated, always the majority as far as numbers
go, though they can never see beyond the end of
their personal nose, and hope only for the swift
gain of a little personal advantage?

Could we, in fact, make any arrangement for
ourselves, worse than that?

XLV

IT is delightful to be back here in Cambridge after so long. The years seem to fall away, and one can almost imagine oneself again an Undergraduate on the threshold of life. I had not realised that the place would grip me so. There I spent three happy years, so full of friendships, of fun and work, and to-day they all come trooping back to me, together with memories of all my fine hopes and intentions. My preposterous dreams.

Well, perhaps it will be a sorry day for the world when the young men cease from dreaming, and from seeing unlikely and hopeful visions, so I do not laugh very much at the ambitions and intentions of that purposeful young man who was once myself.

Cambridge is as beautiful as ever, with all its old cloisters and lawns and chapels. Sometimes I have told myself the charm of it lay in my own youth, and memory. That is not so. It is even more pleasant than it has been all these years in my mind. Even in the early and cold days of spring, it has a welcoming and kindly air. I have walked alone about those still gardens, and through well remembered places. Here is a charming and a quiet life, so far removed from the uncomfortable bustle of every day as to be almost another world.

John met me, much grown, quite a man. He took me up to his rooms, strangely enough on the same staircase as my old ones. There at last I met face to face, your David.

Lady Sahib, I congratulate you on your son. I find in him all the kindly charm that was his Mother's, that easiness of manner that makes one feel entirely at home, and causes one to forget that one is slightly hampered over here because of having a black face. He has such a beautiful laugh, in which I must always join. And over all I notice too a certain thoughtfulness that is strange in somebody still so young.

He dined with us and was immensely gay and amusing and makes us laugh all the time, and over the table I see my son regarding him as a small boy might who is suddenly elevated and invited to have dinner and become friends with Lord Nelson, or perhaps the Duke of Wellington.

A very charming young man indeed, and you are fortunate. He combines marked ability with that charm of personality that would have taken him far even without it. I shall watch with great interest his career. He spoke with much affection of my poor country, and is so confident, so hopeful for everything, so full of plans.

I hear him and my own son talking, and I am for a while young again, and almost I am convinced that all they hope for is possible and can be.

He has been so very kind to my John, who because of him is now accepted in many places he could not have entered alone, just as I myself always got a welcome in any Club I entered with Mr. Chelston.

What a wonderful thing if their hopes could be realised and they may work together in India. This is what they have planned, and indeed to hear these two young men talk, I cannot tell you how easy, how pleasant and how hopeful the future becomes!

For my other son, I am often worried and anxious in mind, and wish I was not so far from home. He does not settle down and sends me from time to time wild letters. He also would fashion a new heaven and a new earth, but not in the way any sensible person could approve of. I have written him only this week, suggesting he takes leave and joins us here, to come for a little while under a more benign influence than at present. As I have pointed out to my son, who now moves with the National Party, to abolish anything before you have something that is as good, if not better, to put in its place, is like abandoning the only available water supply before a fresh well has been located.

He, too, is immensely enthusiastic and hopeful, but has for the moment no wise hand to guide these youthful passions into right channels. I hope he will manage somehow to join us here. How good for him would be his brother John, and your David.

It is a touching thing, this immoderate hopefulness of youth, for evil or for good. I think myself that most of the great things a man achieves have first of all been planted in these wild years of adolescence, before cold reason turned any damper on. In these days my damper is much on, I fear.

I meet many Undergraduates, and one of them asked me very seriously:

"Mr. Nehra, do you suppose that Gandhi is kind to his goat?"

In the eyes of many people here, India is nothing but Gandhi, a sort of easy joke. I put him off with amiable platitudes and assurances as to humanitarian feelings, for how can one discuss such sad complexities over a cup of tea?

I have spent much time looking at all the photographs in David's rooms, in which I get a glimpse at many phases of your life I know nothing of, and see you in so many different surroundings and different aspects. It seems you have changed very little, so that even at the most recent photograph I looked, I knew instantly it was you, just as I first remember you. It took me back to the beginning, and for a moment I was the shy young Indian student beside the door, who wished the floor might swallow him, until he looked up and saw you coming over the room so kindly. And I remembered so clearly those old days, and the joy I had when my first letter brought an unexpected answer from you.

XLVI

To-day being Sunday, I went not to one, but to two Churches, for in London they do God just as magnificently from the point of view of Temples and Pagodas, as the less enlightened folk upon the muddy banks of the rivers of the East.

London amazes me with the complexities of its Churches, Chapels, Meeting Houses, rooms and gatherings. Always they fascinate me greatly, and I remember how as a young man, I was astonished to discover how closely the religious rituals of the West resemble some of our own, when I heard the congregation invited to come and eat the flesh and drink the blood.

Through all religions there runs, oddly this same idea. Through all religions there runs the same tendency to observe the letter of the law without keeping its spirit. To-day I attended a Church where a Bishop spoke, in much purple and fine linen, and on the chest of the Bishop, a most beautiful jewelled cross was hung.

Later I watch this Bishop depart for home in

the glory of a Rolls Royce, with a wife on whose bosom sits many a pearl. . . . Yet the Christian commandment is to consider the lilies, to take no thought of the morrow, to sell all that one has and give it to the poor. Is not Gandhi himself, perhaps, a little closer to that ideal than this Lord Bishop, who perhaps sometimes considers the lilies now and again, but farther does not go?

Inside this Church are many, many old ladies. There is a feminine flavour about all religious establishments in town, for the man who showed me into my seat also wore a petticoat.

The church bell rang for a long time, but it did not draw a great many people out of their houses round the Square. Not as many as sundown would have called to the prayer-mat on the banks of the Hoogli.

At three o'clock I took myself to Westminster Abbey, which is a place I have always loved greatly. I was fortunate enough to obtain a place in the choir stalls, probably because the person with a black stick and brass trimmings on it thought I was someone of more importance than I am.

Like some beautiful dream is Westminster Abbey, and the voice of the organ there echoes as if indeed it was music from another world we heard. Very beautiful are the carvings and the distances, although near at hand there are for my taste too many statues. I can never get it out of my head in Westminster Abbey, that if I could march up to the Altar and peep behind that golden table and embossed screen, there I would see the God of London, a jealous God, wearing the same uniform that is worn on State occasions by His Excellency the Governor of Bengal.

I like so much the scarlet robes of the choir boys, and their white frills and linen, and the golden lights upon the Altar that strike in my heart a certain peace, and awe, I do not know why. I like the dignity with which all the old gentlemen file in, carrying the mortar-board in the hand.

They must, it seems, be shown to their places by the man with the brass-trimmed stick. Even the Canon who went up to read the lesson, was shown the way, and I am aware that this, like the knocking on the door because it was once closed, is another custom. Perhaps once a gentleman started off to read the lessons, and wandering, got lost amongst the statues and memorials, and was never seen again! And ever since that day, they have to take great care. It intrigued me greatly to notice that when the benign old gentleman left his stall to read the lesson, he took also his mortar-board with him, lest in the meantime it be done away with.

The lights were then turned low, and we arrived at the sermon. Very learned is this Worthy Doctor on whom I have looked. Great wisdom has fallen from his lips, and he has said aloud what only comes into my head as a secret fear that it is not for me to voice—that the days draw near filled with evil, and that men are slowly becoming destroyed by the grindings of a machinery they have conceived themselves.

Alas, all of this has been lost, because with the turning down of the lights a great stupor has fallen upon the congregation and they sleep. Behind me is a lady openly enjoying a snore. A stone Crusader with folded hands has a stone seat beside him, on which two Vergers sit, nursing their black and brass sticks, sleeping as soundly as he, the collection-bags waiting between them, and I thought how strange it is that only the Crusader will not be awakened in time for the collection.

It is a pity they do not listen to this learned Doctor. Perhaps it would be better if they did not turn down the lights.

But so it is the world over when the Masters speak. The people sleep and will not hear.

In all your churches I notice very few young men, and this surprises me. With us, the young men must attend church regularly. The heathen are very strict about these matters, because it is in the hands of the young men that the future lies. But all the young men I find are congregated out in the open air, in small bundles in the neighbourhood of the Marble Arch. Here also they are talking about the betterment of Mankind, but there are at least two dozen bundles, and each leader of each bundle has a different good idea.

At these Conferences, as at other Conferences, it seems to me they arrive little further, because there is once again too much of everything. We suffer here from a great over-production of excellent notions.

In a very small space of time I have listened to a Russian gentleman, an Indian of very low caste, some Socialists, and one Communist, all telling the world how to do it, whilst near at hand stood the ever-watchful Policeman, his way of doing it hanging at his girdle in case anyone growing excited wishes to start the improvements at once.

In England to-day nobody minds what you say. To talk, it is encouraged, freely and fully. But if you should do even a very little, that is a breach of the peace, and the Policeman un-hooks his truncheon.

Only with one young man in this great out-of-doors meeting-house have I any sympathy, and he looked a nice young man. He had a pleasant voice, not shouting or excited, and he sheltered beneath a banner called the Income Tax Payers' Association, and talked of how the law-abiding and hard-working and self-respect-ing people are to-day penalized for the not so good. How your better castes cannot afford to have large families any more, because they must from their incomes pay largely to support the offspring of the improvident and feeble minded, the criminal lunatics and incurably diseased, and your on-the-Dole people who find it pays just as well to do nothing as to work.

I cannot help agreeing with this nice young man upon his tub, for this is what strikes me, who am a foreigner, and I cannot see that it is a good idea.

You will have read before you get this, how our Conference progresses but not too fruitfully. There are many views put forward, and many fine speeches made. But always behind it I find myself wondering a little. This Cousin of mine who has set himself up as a Pundit and a physician for many American Ladies in New York, when I once asked him did he really believe that the Lotus seat meant to these people anything at all, replied, "That can one not say, but at least it does them no harm, and gives them something with which to fill their leisure."

And to me it seems all these Conferences serve very nicely to keep us busy and fill in our leisure and absorb energies, until something happens to settle for ever knotting questions.

I am to tour England with several others, visiting the Midlands and the North, also Liverpool. I shall see something of Industrial conditions over here, which will be interesting to me, who have not been further North than Cambridge.

XLVII

ONCE more I shall write you about churches, for I have visited Liverpool Cathedral, and have not yet quite recovered from this experience. Here again the mind of man has conceived something so colossal that the money to complete it remains as yet in the clouds and the pockets of those who it is hoped may soon make a voluntary contribution. I wonder whether you yourself have ever been here, Lady Sahib?

So high, so vast, is this erection, that once inside it I have the unpleasant sensation of being a small ant crawling upon a large surface in dread of a passing foot to crush me.

Beautiful it certainly is, but the beauty is too large for me to admire. It lacks the old and mellow charm of Westminster, and of St. Paul's. I do not feel that behind the reredos and screen here I shall see the God of the English sitting in a suitable uniform. I feel behind I shall come upon nothing but the latest kind of filing cabinet and docketing apparatus and some business-like maps indicating the way to heaven.

Whilst standing there I am reminded in a curious way of those temples buried in the jungle in Ankor, about which I have written to you before. They also were large and magnificent, and in the end had to be abandoned, no one knows why. But may it not have been that there also the erections of the then civilization became unwieldy, became top-heavy and too expensive, and so was abandoned, and presently the bitter karela grew and seeded, and covered it all?

These were my thoughts as I wandered about Liverpool Cathedral which is not yet finished because there is, for the time at least, not enough money.

It was the hour that twilight falls. It falls a little earlier in Liverpool, they tell me, because of the fog and the smoke and the rain. I stood and looked where vistas of carved seats lost themselves in the growing darkness. I wondered would there ever be worshippers enough to fill this great place, since in London so many of the Churches are empty. Out of the shadows appeared a small and benign gentleman wearing dark cloth riding breeches which signify the Priesthood. He said to me:

"Would you like to see it lighted up?"

I waited, much intrigued to know how he, who

was so small and alone, could cause this miracle. He stepped on to the beginning of the Altar steps, and looking up, he said to the black immensity of the ceiling:

"The lights, if you please."

Immediately they went on. He inspected them very thoughtfully and was satisfied with the effect, continuing at once:

"Now the chancel. Left . . ."

It also occurred. He regarded them with a fanciful air, like one arranging flowers, and then, as Moses may have done when he also waited upon his God, looked up once more and said:

"One more in the Transept now."

That also was vouchsafed. Like a man in a dream stood I, attendant on this miracle, and knew not with whom I had fallen in. With the lights, the great spaces filled with shadows became beautiful and rather awful, and nowhere could I see anyone, save this small elderly gentleman and myself.

I murmured my admiration and thanks to my unknown friend. He remarked that it was nothing, and stepping forward once more, looked up and said:

"Thank you *so* much."

At which the lights went off, one by one, and

the miracle was concluded. My companion departed and became one with the shadows that filled the eerie darkness beyond the arches. I remained alone, looking up. I see nothing, neither do I hear any sound to help me realize how it has been done. If an electrician was there, I prefer to believe it was not so, and that I have been privileged to fall in with one whom even the lights obey.

I went out, a little bemused with miracles, into the rain again, and found a cold wind, and the street lamps shivering in it. At the foot of the enormous steps is one young man, broken and shivering also. His eyes haunt me very much, and he asked me for a little money to get some hot tea.

Here we stay in a very fine hotel, all marble within. It is like the pleasure Dome that was built by Kubla Khan, and to continue the likeness is also full of people prophesying wars! The shipping industry is in a sad way, I am told. Unemployed parade everywhere in the streets. But now I find a great paradox. Many people who would employ labour are debarred from so doing, because the wages asked are more than can be afforded. And the dole, they say, is higher than a low wage, and why should a man work and exert himself, for what he can now get for nothing?

Of the many complexities of civilization I had no idea until I came West.

I am so glad to know you are happy in your strange new life. It interests me much to hear what you say of the Chinese, and I have purchased some books about them, including one of Chinese Poems.

One I must tell you, in case you have not met it. It is called *On the Birth of His Son,* and was written in the year 1036 or thereabouts.

> Families, when a child is born
> Want it to be intelligent.
> I, through intelligence
> Having wrecked my whole life
> Only hope the baby will prove
> Ignorant and stupid.
> Then he will crown a tranquil life
> By becoming a Cabinet Minister.

Might that not have been written last week, Lady Sahib? It is a little upsetting to know that so long ago men were wise, and yet it has availed them nothing.

XLVIII

HERE I am in Glasgow, and Glasgow is almost as busy with riots as Bombay. Indeed, it is obvious that whether you have Home Rule, or whether you do not have Home Rule, there is always some excuse for breaking heads, and the ever-ready brickbat flies as enthusiastically here at home, as in the National cause in the East.

The more I travel around, the more certainly do I arrive at the conclusion that England has her caste system and communal troubles just as we have. The bitterness existing between different classes, different schools of thought, what is it but the same difference as lives between our Hindus, and Mohammedans, and our Castes—but wearing a different hat, Lady Sahib! So far they have not all flown at one another's throats, it is true. They are just saying how much they would like to.

Glasgow I find ugly as a nightmare. I am glad we remain here only a little time, because I am unable to speak the language of these people.

In Dundee—and here there is also a riot.

Brickbats fly busily in Dundee. There have this morning been two processions. One demanded an increase of wages. The other demanded work, and were processing because they could not obtain work of any kind whatever.

It was when the two processions met in the Market Place that the trouble and the brickbats arose.

To me it appeared very easy to settle this problem.

"Let the men who have no work, take the jobs of the men who have work but are not satisfied, and at once," I said in my great ignorance. "You bring out the nice connection between work and the stomach, and get the situation down from the realms of high flown fancy, to that of stern realities."

That, I am at once informed, is a rotten idea. Trade Unions would not allow it. Yet one would have thought even a Trade Union might perhaps realize that if something does not pay already, it cannot further increase its wages without going bust. And perhaps—there is no saying—if everyone worked very hard and tried their best, some concerns might find it possible, later on, to pay higher wages they cannot arrive at now. This is how it appeared to me, a stranger and an onlooker. But they tell me I am wrong. For always, it seems, there are those who wish to grind the face of the poor. And the poor, naturally, is not prepared to present the face for this grinding.

Yet I have met many people from whose conversation one would not gather them to be grinders, and again I am convinced that mainly this trouble also is talk.

In Dundee I had some conversation with a gentleman who tells me that shortly he hopes to come out to India to assist her in her struggle for Home Rule. He said that India must not allow herself to be browbeaten. That she must take a firm line.

"So," said I, "you believe in Direct Action, both at home and abroad."

"Assuredly."

"In non-co-operation?"

"What else?"

"Perhaps even in assassinations?"

He was enthusiastic on the subject of assassinations, and said of a certainty they were often necessary. The downtrodden, he said, must instantly arise.

"And see to it that they down-tread somebody else?" said I.

"Yes," said he. "No," hastily said he. What he meant was, everyone should throw off the hand of the oppressor.

"But Dundee," said I, "has long since thrown off the hand of the oppressor, has she not? And what about Dundee? To me, she appears sorely afflicted with a visitation of brickbats at this very moment?"

That, he said, was different. They were now trying to throw off the yoke of Capitalism. He gave me many figures, which I fancy were mostly wrong, and quoted Russia. He said the whole world was looking to Russia to point the path to freedom.

"At one time, my friend," I said to him, "the whole of India looked to the British Raj to point the path to freedom. Now they endeavour to throw it off!"

At which this man became a little impatient with me, and would not agree that even in Russia all men were not happy and satisfied with their surroundings. They were being taught how to be, he said. The time was coming when all men, black, white, and yellow, would dwell together in unity.

I said to my new friend sadly enough, "Since people of the same nationality and even members of one family can rarely dwell for any time together in unity, your Utopia appears to me remote as a complete change in the heart of man."

He said that was not so. Later it emerges that he is paid a weekly salary by some Society to go round stirring people up to take action against their wrongs.

What a bad idea. Unless people have wrongs, he must hastily invent some or he may lose his salary.

I told him candidly we did not require his assistance in India. It made me sad, remembering the harm that has been done to my own son, Arvind, by just this kind of foolish and wild talk, subsidised by some wild-cat Society for the overthrow of everything.

After that, he has grown cold towards me, and said since I was only a nigger, what could I possibly know about anything at all? There is a large community here in England to whom there exists only two kinds of coloured people.

One is Nigger—the other, Chink!

So I was glad to get away from Dundee's saddened streets, where it rains so much and so unhelpfully, and so many white women have plucked me by the sleeves. So ugly were most of them—so bedraggled and so thin. I can hardly believe that for a moment they are able to hope to raise any money upon their appeal to any man.

What a dismal letter! My next one to you shall be of nothing whatever but cheerfulness. From here I go to Edinburgh and everybody tells me that is a beautiful and a clean place, so let us hope from it I shall communicate only good and helpful news!

Yours to me came with a packet of papers from my London Hotel and cheered me up very much. It is, as you say, hard to see China's way out of her troubles. One can see that for these colossal armies she has, there is nothing unless they go on fighting.

And like Sir Nigel Hill, they must live.

XLIX

FOR your wires, and for your kindness in this my darkest hour, I shall not even try to thank you beyond saying they have helped me more than anything else has, to bear this terrible time.

I must now write you fully about it. There is no one in my own small world to whom I can talk of it with any certainty of being understood. In a way I feel that the shadow has fallen also on me, of what has occurred, and to a certain extent it is a barrier even with my own kind over here on the Conference. The newspapers have also got hold of it, and ask, "Why is this man in Government Employ?"

I was in London, leaving the Conference one evening when I got the news. I was planning to return home via Germany, and thinking peacefully enough of my plans when first I saw, carried on the stomach of a newspaper seller, a Poster.

"Governor of the Northern Provinces Assassinated," it said. Horrified as you may imagine, I bought a paper, and learn it is my own son, my first-born son Arvind, who has done this thing.

He has announced that it is for India's freedom he has struck a blow. He lies, I hear, in the Hospital, because he has tried also to shoot himself.

It was some little time before I could believe it. All night I walked the bedroom floor, stopping only now and then to read the paper, to see if it is true that I have seen there what I think I have seen. For how can I believe my own son would do this thing? All night I wait, hoping for a telegram to say it is not so, that it is a mistake.

And in the morning the telegram has come, and it is true.

I can remember really very little of my leaving England, or the voyage back here. It was a nightmare journey in which I sat much alone, to be pointed out discreetly as the Father of the latest assassin—indeed a *rôle* I had little expected ever to be forced to play in this life.

So I arrived at Bombay, and was met there by my daughter in great sorrow, who told me everything.

For a long time I knew well my son Arvind had been under the influence of the less wise of

India's prophets, the more fiery of India's un-controlled and undisciplined youth. But I thought, "At heart this boy is sound. He will outgrow." In my letters to him I have always exhorted reasonableness.

Now I cannot blame myself enough for not taking seriously that which was indeed serious, for expecting to pass clouds that only gathered thicker, until they obscure daylight.

I found my son in Hospital up country—my first-born son, little more now than skin and bone. An old man, my son of twenty-four, so that I have difficulty in believing this is my son.

Beside his bed, two Punjabi policemen, bearded and heavy both of person and of wit. Stupid, though a little sorry for us, with the faces of bewildered sheep.

Arvind whispered to me, "It is all right, Father. You must not worry. I have struck a blow for freedom and now I shall die."

What can I say to him? What can experience ever say to misguided youth? Only I can weep. "My son, my son," I told him. "This is no blow for freedom you have struck, but one more nail in the coffin of India."

I begged of the Policemen to leave us for a little while that I can talk to my son. But this they refuse to do, since my son is a Police case, and therefore they must remain with him all the time.

And now there comes to me out of my present gloom some small rays of brightness. For first, I find the Senior Police Officer here is known to me from the past, and when I go to see him, kindness and compassion is on his face. He at once gave orders that when I visit my son, the Policemen can remain without upon the veranda, for this same Police Officer worked with me many years ago in Myosein and has not forgotten me.

"I am damned sorry for this," he said to me. "It is a terrible thing for you. The best thing that can happen to the boy now . . ."

He did not finish what he was going to say, but I know very well what it is, and that he means it would be best for my son that he does not recover but dies.

Meanwhile the Doctors and Nurses are doing all they can to bring him back to life, so that they may find out he has done what we all know he has done, and so kill him again.

In some of her aspects, is Justice not like the tiger of the Jungle, who, having got a man into her clutches, will let him crawl a little way towards safety, will allow him to arrive at the very outskirts of escape, and then pounce again!

By the great kindness of this Police Officer, I can now speak with my son quietly and in peace, and so I learnt from him all about this horrible affair and how it has come that he has shot Sir Nigel Hill.

We have, repeated over again, just the story of my youth. My early difficulties in settling down and finding my place, the same smarts and indignities, but falling here on one with more fire in the heart, more initiative, perhaps more courage than ever I have had. Attributes which, rightly handled, Lady Sahib, surely would have worked for some good!

"He was so much hated by all . . ." my son told me. "There were so many injustices, indignities, and heart-burnings. We of the Society drew lots. The lot fell to me, and what else could I do, Father? I have struck for freedom a blow that had to be struck."

Then I could only weep and say, "Foolish boy, do you not understand that in this world there is no freedom? That men can only exchange one bondage for another, until the heart of man is changed?"

"You have worked with him as a young man

also," said my son. "You know. Tell me this, did you find it easy? Could you bear all the coldness, the insults, the sneers? Are we dogs to be treated so—to be scorned and passed over?"

What could I say to my son, Lady Sahib, remembering clearly as I do my own bitterness? Has it not perhaps been in my heart still when this little boy was born, and so passed on by me to him? Why did I not avail myself of the opportunity that was mine, so many years ago, to rid the world of this man quietly and efficiently, for the sum of Rs.55 as was in my power? In my heart is that old, old cry:

"Would God that I had died for thee, O Absalom, my son."

So we have some quiet days together, talking little of what has happened, since what avails much talk now? We returned together into the past when we were peaceful and happy, a family undivided. And always I hope one morning I shall come and hear that he has died quietly whilst asleep, since for my son there is no hope but this.

Together we returned into his childhood. He holds my hand, and for a little while the assassination is forgotten and I am together with my son.

Then one day comes to me the Doctor, and tells me all is well, and my son will recover.

It seems to me that the anguish I have been through is nothing to the anguish that still must come, as I watch the cumbersome wheels of the law take my son and grind him to powder. Now that I have been with my son, have spoken with him, the sense I had hoped of old would save him, has awakened, and he cries to me:

"Father, what have I done. Why did I listen to them? Indeed, I was mad. . . ."

To the Doctor I said, "So you will mend my son, only to break him anew?"

"We must do our duty," was his reply.

Then in my despair I went to the Head Superintendent in supreme charge of this Hospital, in his office in headquarters, and here in my gloom comes another ray of light. For I find it is Colonel Shawn, the same man I have known so many years ago in Calcutta, to whom I have been grateful for many courtesies and friendlinesses of old.

Do you see, Lady Sahib, how all the threads of life begin to weave a pattern?

I have talked a long time with Colonel Shawn, have told him all, and of this Society, and the pamphlets that came from England, turning the heart of my son from wisdom with fine words and high-sounding promises. Those to whom of old we looked for guidance, what message do they send to our young men to-day? Our young men, who still follow a cause, even the wrong cause, to death?

"And now," I told him, "they say my son will recover. Can we do nothing, so that he does not recover? How can I bear that which still lies before me if my son gets well?"

Colonel Shawn stood in silence beside the window, his back to me for some time.

"I wish to God I could help you," he said. Then for some minutes he looked at me thoughtfully. He said I must take care of myself, since if I also get ill, what will it avail?

I said, "How can I be well, who can neither eat nor sleep?"

He said, "I shall give you something, Arvind, that will help you to sleep," and he requested me to come later and see him in his office, which I did, and was there given by him a small bottle.

"You must be careful," he told me, "not to take more than two of these tablets, because an overdose, and you would continue to sleep and awake no more."

What peace and rest is there for me, even

through medicines, I say to myself, when to sleep is only to forget for a little while, and then awake and remember my first-born who has brought this shame and terror upon us, and must shortly stand in the Dock, and receive a sentence I myself have so often given to other malefactors.

L

YOUR messages have helped me so much in these terrible days. And for the kindness and thoughtfulness of those about me here, I cannot be grateful enough.

Arvind continues to improve. Such is the tragic vitality of youth. Within a month, they tell me, he will be well enough to stand his trial and be brought before the Magistrates. In the eyes of the Police Officer who told me this, I read a great compassion, and he said:

"I wish the boy hadn't pulled through at all. It would have been so much easier for everyone."

For me now the worst part of it all is that I read in Arvind's eyes only terror and remorse and fear. He clings to my hand, like my small son of so long ago. He says many times to me:

"I was mad, Father. I was mad. I became so angry, reason was dead. To think that I, your son, should so bring shame on to our name."

To-night Colonel Shawn, who comes up often himself to see me, and in his own quiet way has been so thoughtful, and so kind, arrived after the hour of the last Dressings. I took him by the arm and led him out onto the small veranda. I was not ashamed to weep before him, for he also is the father of sons at home in England, and knows the tug at the heart when evils threatened the first-born.

Perhaps I have been distraught and hardly aware of what I am saying, when I besought him:

"Can you do nothing for this my son, so that he dies now quietly for his sins, and without further torture? Truly my son has seen the evil of what he has done, and received punishment enough?"

He looked at me very kindly, and laid the hand on my shoulder.

"What can I do? I have no other course but my duty here. God knows no one would be gladder than I would, if you came to me to-morrow morning and told me your son was dead."

"If there is any mercy in your heart," I implored him, "not as from Englishman to Indian, or one official to another official, but because you are also the father of sons, can you not help me that he suffers no more?"

"What can I do for you, that I have not already done," asked Colonel Shawn. "It is a beastly and an unreliable business, and you have my deep sympathy, but I fear I cannot help you any more." Then he looked at me, and he asked me was I taking the tablets he gave me.

Yes, I told him. I took them.

"They make you sleep quietly?"

"Yes," I told him. "They bring me a little rest at nights."

"You must not forget, Arvind, to be careful with them," he said. "Because three or four of them would be a fatal dose, and if you took so many you would continue to sleep and never wake up any more. . . ." He said this, and then he added, very gently. "It is a most quiet and peaceful death, without any pain."

And after that he went away.

It is because my wits are so heavy and dulled with misery I have not seen before. It is not until this evening it came to me in a flash and was made clear that all the Colonel Sahib could do for me under these circumstances he had already done, putting a weapon into my hands. Now justice has become tempered with Mercy.

I understand at least what it is he has said to

me, without saying anything, who is also the father of sons and so has in his heart pity beyond his official duties, for that which is young and broken past all mending.

LI

My son has died in his sleep, very quietly and without pain, and now is gone where no doubt he will work out expiation for his errors in this life.

Nothing is now left to me of my first-born, save a grave by which to stand and remember old days, when he played with me and told me how like a frog I looked in my spectacles.

It is over and finished. I have now only one son who once had three. For some time this business must be against John. He is the brother of an Assassin—and whenever he comes up for promotion, somebody will remember that fact and make a Note upon a margin.

He will live it down. *Toute passe—l'amitie reste,* as the French say.

It is a comfort to me to know he will always have a good friend in your David. For him life will be easier, because he found his Mr. Chelston in good time.

He has written me, over this affair, such kind and such charming letters.

On the day after my son's funeral, my daughter, who is now married, brought forth her first son. One departs and another arrives, and so the old world goes on, the same story told, and retold, as nursery tales are told to children.

I have written to the family of Sir Nigel Hill, of my sorrow and my distress, and to my surprise receive back from his mother such a kind and such an understanding letter, with nothing of bitterness and nothing at all of blame.

Here and there in the darkness, Lady Sahib, a little gleam. A small light.

LII

Now I am returned to the old home to where I was a boy. Upon the house-top in the evening, I hear my daughter sing to her son, the childish tune my mother has often sung to me:

"*Are, Koko, ja re, Koko!*"

All the day long in my garden, the pigeons cry softly "*Haq sirr hu. . .*" which we understand to be "God knows the secret," and indeed I find much comfort, now, in this gentle and persistent assurance.

The house is quite unchanged, the women's apartments full of much tawdry stained glass which to me once was very beautiful. On the flat roof my servants turn punctually to pray at sunset, and the view I see from my window is the one my opening eyes first beheld.

The march of time has taken me round in a circle, and here I am, home again. So many dreams unfulfilled, so many hopes proved barren. The new Heaven and earth I looked for, more distant than ever it was.

And here I sit, in my old home of my youth,

aware that even now I have not quite abandoned all my dreams. Some shreds of them I still draw about me, like a cloak in the evening. Hopes that spring, not for myself, no longer for my dear first-born son who is no more—but for young John.

So we live again in our children, and because of them can never entirely die. This for me is immortality enough, should there be no other.

Naturally we are now entirely cast off from those circles in which once we moved, because of my son's sin. Those friends who still come to visit me, do so secretly. Not, they point out to me, because they personally believe I have ever been other than entirely loyal and against assassinations, "but what," they say, "would the officials in my department think, if it got about that I came to talk with you, my dear fellow. After all, I have got to live, and though I know, and you know, that all this is nonsense, the small man in the village, and the little man beside the tank—he knows something quite different!"

So I live by myself a great deal, and all I ask is for peace, and the society of my children and of my grandchildren, and your punctual and kindly letters that keep me still in a world from which I am now cast out.

Boycotts continue. Talks continue. There is in Bengal a veritable reign of terror. I hear of it all from afar, and am not drawn into its turmoil who sit now apart in my garden in the cool day.

From afar, how grotesque and how comical much of this masque appears. New Delhi complete, and now a party wishes to cut the Viceroy's salary so that he could hardly afford to live in one room on it. In this world of to-day there are too many of these grand buildings, too many frozen assets and pretty playthings that cannot pay their way. We have played such a beautiful game, but behold, it is too expensive. We cannot afford it. All the world over this cry reaches the heavens. We must abandon our Fairy-lands and pull up our socks, and get back to realities.

Wars, and rumours of wars, and still the Peace Conference at Geneva, burbling like a sweet music heard from afar, never clearly enough for any tune to be distinguished, so that one cannot tell, like the Old Lady of Sheen, whether it is indeed 'God Save the Weasel' they play, or 'Pop Goes the Queen'.

My small grandson grows and brings much

gladness to my house. He has very black curls, and reminds me so much of Arvind that I, now growing old, think it is my own first-born who climbs up on to my knee. And sometimes, hearing the patter of his small feet upon the house-top, I find myself thinking, "My son is up there, at play," and for a moment fail to remember the time that is gone.

My daughter will have her next child in the Monsoon. Already, like her mother, she becomes distressingly stout.

Unlike the sister who is now a Doctor, this daughter is not at all emancipated. She is satisfied to remain at the home, and have many children, leaving the ruling of the world to the men folk, busying herself only with things that pertain to the house.

In my lifetime I have seen many women, of many lands, and it has led me to wonder whether after all, the cloistered women of this country are to be only and entirely pitied. I have seen the beautiful and accomplished women of the West, working so hard at some profession, and endeavouring at the same time to attend to the home, and becoming by it all a little worn out. I have met one Englishwoman of some culture who said to me:

"Tell your women they have not got so much to complain of, peacefully in their Zenana," and at first I think she is making a pleasantry, until somebody has told me she works very hard indeed through many years, to keep some children, also a husband who does nothing, only plays golf.

Every system has its own particular ills, and I wonder now, if any particular ill is much worse than some other? For what, after all, does it profit a woman to be clever and very beautiful in the morning of her life—when the end of it arrives?

In time she, also, must grow old, perhaps with many stomachs and chins. In age, it is the memory of dear kindnesses, of duties steadfastly performed, of watchings in sickness, that make for happiness and engenders the love that does not die.

From your David I have such amusing and delightful letters. These have become some of my chief pleasures, and often he consults me about this and that to do with his work, and tells me of the strange things he comes across. . . . John is to be drafted up next Cold Weather, as his assistant.

So one at least of my dreams has not come to nothing at all.

I sit much upon the house-tops. From there I see the river, and some distant hills. Also the Towers of Silence, with those dark birds always about them.

Just now the whole world shimmers in the heat, and is dry and dusty with the haze of the Hot Weather. In my garden the coppersmith bird continues diligently his monotonous occupation.

I suppose it is no very inspiring view. Yet to me it is more well beloved than many of the green vistas of more beautiful parts of the world.

I am aware of its shortcomings—but it was my childhood.

LIII

I DESERVE your reproaches in part only. Indeed, I have not forgotten you. Upon my desk here stands always the small snapshots of an English lady, and a very small boy, together with the later and beautiful picture you sent me at Christmas-time, and the one of your David, laughing down at a small dog, with, in his mouth, his pipe.

I am pleased to think of you again in England, so that when David and John get leave, you will be there, and they will see you. For John will go to England also. He has much zeal for learning, and when listening to him, almost am I young again, starting out on to the threshold of life also, full of much hope.

But I do not start, Lady Sahib. On the other hand, I probably finish. For now I must tell you that for some time I have not been very well. For some time I have been aware all was not right within, but like many much more enlightened persons than myself, for as long as possible I put off any enquiries into this unpleasant matter, lest I learn that which is not agreeable.

Recently I make an effort, and I do learn that which is not agreeable! It is, indeed, worse than I had thought. The chassis has developed a body squeak!

"In youth," says the Chinese Poet, "man is a prey to an hundred desires. In age, to a thousand diseases."

I have to face an operation.

It has been some sort of a battle to settle the old women, who would have me turn to the Ayervedic Doctors of our own kind. Indeed, they are ready and waiting to brew me a concoction of bats' wings and saliva of swallows caught at the seashore which, they aver, will at once remove the cause of my distress!

I have waived this unattractive mixture, and go into the Hospital to-morrow morning.

I cannot say I greatly care. No man lives for ever, and certainly I have collected a good experience of joys and sorrows, hopes and disappointments, to take with me from this world to wherever it is I must at last go—and through it all friendship runs like a golden thread. When there has been this golden thread, how can we complain.

[251]

For us there is held out no promise of green fields, no crystal seas beside which we may sit, harping continuously. What an odd conception of Heaven that has always seemed to me, and how out of keeping with the men for whom it has been arranged!

For your average man-in-the-street, Lady Sahib, though sometimes able to make much distressing sound upon a barrel-organ—what would he do with a harp? Or what, indeed, with a field however Celestial, if devoid of any Public House in view anywhere?

Often watching His Honour the Chief Justice performing in the High Courts in Bombay, I have endeavoured to imagine him also in this predicament, and am forced to the conclusion that when his time came he also would harp unhandily.

Is it not strange that for a race so prone to work only for an advantage, and the ready takers of all kinds of bribes and rewards, our religion holds out to us none. No hope have we of everlasting joys to abound, or that all tears will be washed from our faces, or even, alas, that Father, Mother, Child and Sister, will ever meet again in rural and musical surrounding.

Of all your English hymns I have listened to,

one only has aroused some answering cord in the heart of me, who am a black man. I do not know who wrote it, but I heard it first in a small country church to which I had walked over pleasant fields, at evening. It begins with the words "O Love, that will not let me go", but the verse that remains most constant in my mind is this one:

> O joy, that seekest me through pain,
> I cannot close my heart to thee!
> I trace the rainbow through the rain
> And feel the promise is not vain
> That morn shall tearless be.

Vaguely, and in some way I cannot tell you, I also feel the promise is not in vain, although the Faith in which I was brought up gives us small guidance on that matter.

For us there is only another life, and after that another, increasing in worthiness only in due ratio to our present endeavour. I must, as yet, live many lives before my circle is complete, and so at least I have this hope. That in some future existence, returning perhaps when men have long ago buried their differences as to hats, customs, creeds, and methods of burials, we shall meet again, you and I who have in our strange fashion been such friends, and you will say:

"There is a friend of mine, whom once I knew
with a darkened face."

To-morrow evening they will operate, and
perhaps I shall die, and that is the truth of this
matter. I do not care. I am now an old man. I
do not wish to experience any more, to see
anything more, to suffer anything more. It will be
pleasant never again to hear a young girl in a red
hat say of India, in a London Club:

"But how can anyone want to go to India
to-day, when they may at any moment have to
work under a Wog."

It will be pleasant, at least for a little while,
to be still and quiet, and to get some rest. The
thought of death does not in any way distress
me. To die, what is it? In the morning for a
little while the sun shines, and we are glad in
its warmth. But evening must come, and
night. Only the foolish man looks for anything
else.

In this world, where men have fashioned so
many strange gods to comfort them in their
hour of extremity, I know of none I have any
real wish to turn to. But I hope all the most
reliable ones will look after you, and yours, and
bless you with much comfort in your growing

older. I hope also they will see to it that we meet again, in some good place where men have at last laid down the sword—and the fountain pen.

Age has brought to me the conviction that it is the latter which does, in the long run, most harm.

Now it is evening—too dark for me to write to you any more, and so for a little while I must say good-bye. The shadows fall, Lady Sahib. The shadows fall. I must wait until I hear upon the stairs the feet of one come to light my lamp.

A Selected List of Non-Fiction Titles Available from Mandarin

While every effort is made to keep prices low, it is sometimes necessary to increase prices at short notice. Mandarin Paperbacks reserves the right to show new retail prices on covers which may differ from those previously advertised in the text or elsewhere.

The prices shown below were correct at the time of going to press.

All these books are available at your bookshop or newsagent, or can be ordered direct from the publisher. Just tick the titles you want and fill in the form below.

Mandarin Paperbacks, Cash Sales Department, PO Box 11, Falmouth, Cornwall TR10 9EN.

Please send cheque or postal order, no currency, for purchase price quoted and allow the following for postage and packing:

UK including BFPO   £1.00 for the first book, 50p for the second and 30p for each additional book ordered to a maximum charge of £3.00.

Overseas including Eire   £2 for the first book, £1.00 for the second and 50p for each additional book thereafter.

NAME (Block letters) ....

ADDRESS..

....

☐ I enclose my remittance for ....

☐ I wish to pay by Access/Visa Card Number ☐☐☐☐☐☐☐☐☐☐☐☐☐☐☐☐

Expiry Date ☐☐☐☐